don't throw it, GROW IT!

68 WINDOWSILL PLANTS from kitchen scraps

DEBORAH PETERSON & MILLICENT SELSAM

Storey Publishing

I WOULD LIKE TO DEDICATE THIS BOOK POSTHUMOUSLY TO
MILLICENT SELSAM, A WONDERFUL FRIEND AND MENTOR.

The mission of Storey Publishing is to serve our customers by
publishing practical information that encourages
personal independence in harmony with the environment.

Edited by Gwen Steege and Sarah Guare
Art direction and book design by Alethea Morrison
Text production by Liseann Karandisecky

Illustrations by © Chip Wass

Indexed by Andrea Chesman

Printed in the United States by CJK
10 9 8 7 6 5 4 3 2 1

Library of Congress Cataloging-in-Publication Data

Peterson, Deborah.
  Don't throw it, grow it! : 68 windowsill plants from kitchen scraps.
     p. cm.
  Includes index.
  ISBN 978-1-60342-064-8 (pbk. : alk. paper)
  1. Window gardening. 2. House plants—Propagation. 3. Horticultural crops.
  I. Selsam, Millicent E. (Millicent Ellis), 1912–1996. II. Title.
SB419.P415 2008
635—dc22
                                                          2008005519

CONTENTS

CHAPTER 4

plants from herbs and spices 77

CHAPTER 5

plants from latin america 95

CHAPTER 6

plants from asia 121

PReFace

Some thirty years ago, I gave a talk at the Indoor Light Gardening Society of New York, with the title "Eat the Fruit and Plant the Seed." After the talk, a diminutive red-headed lady came up to me and said, "I want to write a book with you." I thought she was probably daft, but I took her card and checked her out. Milly Selsam was not daft, nor was she an inexperienced writer. She was a well-known author of award-winning children's science books.

I said yes to Milly, and so began our horticultural adventure. We were fearless New Yorkers scouring the streets of our city in search of ethnic grocery stores and the unknown fruits and vegetables we might find. Our modus operandi was quite simple: we would choose a particular ethnic neighborhood and search the markets there for an unusual fruit or vegetable. From the Latin markets on the West Side and the Bronx to the Indian groceries on Lexington Avenue, the markets in Chinatown and Little Italy, and the Mediterranean markets in Queens, we covered a lot of territory.

We almost always found something new and different. We would each buy two items: one to eat and one to grow. After that, we'd have lunch in a local restaurant. Some of our "Pit Stop" adventures were hysterical and some were a little scary. Milly would pick up each item and carefully scrutinize it for tell-tale roots, soft spots, budding eyes, or firm flesh. Needless to say, this did not thrill the grocers. I suspect we were cursed in many languages.

Years ago, I went on a field trip with one of my children and spied a box of the most unusual tubers I had ever seen: oval, black, and firm as a potato. Following the agreed method of purchase, I bought two for myself and two for Milly. I left the shop to the usual cries of, "It won't grow, lady." (I must know that expression in six languages.) Undaunted, I dropped the beautiful tubers off at Milly's office. Later that evening Milly called, giggling, and said, "You bought preserved goose eggs, you silly." Some of our most marvelous plants started after a visit to an Asian market; they are well worth a little egg on the kitchen floor.

We continued to meet after the book was published, sharing our love of plants, food, and people until Milly's death in 1987. When revising information on pits for this book, Milly's voice was always in my head.

Much has changed since this book was originally published. Plants that Milly and I considered exotic, such as kiwi, mango, and papaya, are now sold year-round in most supermarkets. The eighties and nineties saw an influx of exotic fruits and vegetables: the malodorous durian from Thailand, the phallic fruit of the cutleaf philodendron, and the sea anemone–lookalike rambutan. This was a wonderful time for a "pit grower" – until a family ate imported strawberries from Guatemala and became dreadfully ill. The U.S. government's response was to irradiate all imported fruits and vegetables. Irradiation changes the plant's DNA and kills the seeds. We have managed to grow an occasional imported mango or papaya, but it is now best to grow only those fruits and vegetables grown in the lower 48 U.S. states, so that you avoid fruits that have been irradiated and are therefore sterile and won't grow.

When I give a pit talk, I always bring a large bowl of mixed fruits and vegetables. I tell the audience that within the bowl there are annuals, perennials, trees, shrubs, and vines that will all grow! There are wonderful surprises in store for you as you use this book. Grab a friend and make a "pit stop"! But remember: Always buy two of each – one to grow and one to eat.

CHAPTER 1

NITTY GRITTY

growing techniques

Join me on a journey both horticultural and gastronomic. This book will show you how to grow plants from the seeds, pits, and roots that you might otherwise discard. I also hope that the book will inspire you to seek out the more unusual fruits and vegetables for planting. Explore local markets, as well as whatever ethnic markets are available to you. I give some direction as to where and when to find some of these unusual plants. If I haven't mentioned availability, you can find the herb, fruit, or vegetable year-round in most supermarkets.

Almost every unprocessed fruit or vegetable can be grown into a decorative houseplant. Some are perennials (those that repeat their growth cycle year after year); others are annuals (plants that complete their growth cycle in one season) or biennials (those that complete the cycle in two years). You will be amazed as you discover how these beautiful plants develop.

1

WHAT PLANTS NEED TO GROW

There is no such thing as a "green thumb." Plants will grow well if you learn the conditions they require and if you provide the correct light, water, fertilizer, and containers filled with a growing medium, such as water, soil, or peat. The secret to successful gardening is mimicking the natural growing conditions of your plant's native habitat.

Some plants, such as mango and almond, will germinate and flourish only under a particular set of environmental conditions. When the mango seed drops to the ground, it lands on warm, moist soil. As soon as the flesh around it rots away, it germinates. The mango plant needs a warm, humid, sunny environment and lots of water year-round to grow. An almond tree drops its leaves in the fall, signaling a period of dormancy, and needs three to four months of temperatures 42°F and below. The almond nut also falls to the ground in autumn, just before a harsh, cold winter. It must stay in its protective shell until spring, when growing conditions are favorable. To successfully grow your mango and almond plants, you must be aware of their natural environment and what that tells you about their requirements.

If you've never grown plants before or need to catch up on some basics, here are some fundamental facts about their growth requirements.

getting the light right

Plants have an incredible ability to manufacture their own food. They do this through a process called *photosynthesis*, whereby the plant cells combine the energy of sunlight, naturally occurring carbon dioxide from the air, and water to form sugars and starches. Consider the beet root. It is full of starch, water, and sugar — all of the food necessary for its growth. With the help of sunlight and air, the plant uses these sugars and starches to grow. It is quite miraculous.

Plants differ in their light requirements. If your plant turns pale green and its stems become very long, giving the plant a leggy appearance, it needs more light. If your plant is getting too much light, the leaves may become scorched or pale yellow in color, even though the plant's food is adequate. For most plants, too much light indoors is rare. Assess your home's sun exposures. Eastern light begins with sunrise and is cool. A southern exposure offers the most hours of sun but it can get too hot. Western light has the slanted sun of the late afternoon and is not as intense. Northern light, so treasured by artists for its steadiness, is the lowest light intensity of the exposures. Each of these exposures is just right for one or more kinds of plants.

In cities, many windows are obstructed by tall buildings that block some or all of the sunlight. Milly and I both lived in New York City when we first met, and we grew plants indoors under lights. Many garden centers and magazines advertise commercial light units. These comprise two to four fluorescent tubes that mimic the ultraviolet rays found in sunlight. These commercial lights can be expensive, but you can build your own light units from fluorescent tubes and fixtures available in any hardware

store. Use a combination of cool and warm white lights. We've installed these light units in empty shelves in bookcases and cupboards and found them to be just as effective as the commercial units.

watering wisdom

Without water, a plant becomes limp and wilts. With too much water, the roots are deprived of the air that they need to keep from rotting. The trick is to keep the soil moist but not too wet. It is impossible to give general rules for all plants, but you can start by watering your plants when the surface of the soil feels dry or the surface of the soil has changed color from dark and moist to a lighter color, indicating dryness. Do not sprinkle a little water on top and leave it at that. Water thoroughly: add water until it seeps out through the hole in the bottom of the pot or container. Then don't water until the surface of the soil feels dry again. It is best to use water that is slightly warm.

Water enters the roots and goes up through the stems into leaves; then, it evaporates through pores in the leaves. It is this transpiration that causes the plant to pull more water up from the roots. The amount of water a plant transpires depends on the thickness of its leaves. Plants with feathery, thin leaves, such as tamarind, lose water rapidly; their soil should be carefully monitored. Plants with thicker leaves, such as avocados, lose much less water through transpiration.

A couple of basics: Plants kept in a cool, moist place dry out more slowly than plants kept in a warm, dry place. Plants in small pots dry out faster than those in large containers.

To combat dry inside air, you can do several things. You can mist the leaves of your plants with a spray bottle, or you can also group your plants on shallow trays filled with pebbles. Add water up to the top layer of pebbles and keep the water at that level at all times. The evaporation of the water in the tray will add moisture to the air because of the extent of the tray's surface area.

Notice your plant's stage of growth. If a plant is actively growing and putting out new leaves and stems or flowers, it needs more water than a plant that appears to have stopped growing. Many plants go through a rest period in winter, at which time they need much less water than they do in the spring, when active growth begins. Of course, checking the soil moisture on a regular basis is one of the secrets to success.

potting up plants

Garden centers and supermarkets offer a wide variety of potting mixes to suit the growing requirements of particular plants. For the plants featured in this book, however, you should simply select a high-quality, all-purpose potting mix. Most bagged mixes are sterile, that is, free of weed seeds and disease organisms.

When plants are growing in the ground, in rich soil that's full of organic matter, they are able to make their own food from carbon dioxide, water, sunlight, and certain chemical elements that naturally occur in soil. The most important of these elements are nitrogen, phosphorus, and potassium. Nitrogen makes leaves and stems grow and stay green. Phosphorus encourages the growth of flowers, fruits, and seeds. Potassium stiffens stems and promotes sturdy, compact growth.

Plants grown in containers, however, need help acquiring these elements. Peat-and-perlite mixes have a very low nutrient content, so you'll need to fertilize your plants in order to supply them with the nutrients they need to grow. You may select a potting mix with a slow-release fertilizer or one that is enriched with compost and organic amendments. In both of these cases, the plant will eventually deplete the supply of nutrients and need to be repotted with fresh mix. A third option is to fertilize regularly with a liquid fertilizer, following the directions on the label.

If you choose a liquid fertilizer, don't get carried away! You can easily burn both the roots and leaves, and kill a plant by overfertilizing. This is especially true in winter, when many plants are not in active growth and do not need to be fertilized. In these cases, it's best to hold the fertilizer until you see signs of new growth in spring. For plants that are actively growing, it's best to fertilize only lightly at first, then increase the amount as necessary.

GETTING PLANTS STARTED

You can start new plants by using various different parts of a parent plant, such as roots, tubers, bulbs, seeds, or cuttings. Different parts of the plant require different growing methods. Start large tubers or seeds and bulbs in water, over pebbles, in soil, or in a sphagnum bag. Small seeds require just one method: soil or peat. In many cases, after you have started your plants, you will transfer the sprouted plants to containers with soil. Some plants, however, are best left in pebbles with water.

In the "How to Grow It" section of each plant entry, you may be referred back to instructions in this section.

starting plants in water

Large tubers, pits, or roots, such as sweet potatoes, daikon, arrowhead, and water chestnuts, can be started in water. Suspend the tuber, pit, or root in water by piercing the flesh or pit with bamboo skewers. (Toothpicks are too weak to hold these plants as they start to grow.) Plants started in water should be transplanted to soil when they have 4 inches of roots. The roots are quite brittle and should be handled with care.

Arrowhead and water chestnuts can be floated in bowls of water until they develop roots that are 4 inches long. Be sure to add charcoal to their water. Use one part "activated charcoal" to four parts water. This helps to keep the water sweet. The charcoal can be purchased in garden or pet centers.

THE SECRET OF THE SPHAGNUM BAG

When Milly and I wanted to start mango from its large seed or taro from its root, we had no idea which end was up and which end was down. We also wanted to create a warm, moist environment, similar to its natural sprouting environment. Our answer was to create a sphagnum bag. This bag can be used for tubers such as malanga, large seeds such as genip, and roots such as taro.

Fill a quart-sized, sealable plastic bag with barely moist, long-grained sphagnum moss. The moss should have the consistency of a good unbaked pie crust and should not drip when squeezed. (Long-grained moss is available at most garden centers; if you can't find any, use regular peat moss.) Place the seed in the bag, making sure it is completely surrounded with the moss. Seal the bag and place it in a warm, dark spot. Check the bag several times a week to make sure there are no soft spots on the tuber or root, or mold on the seed. If it is too dry, add water; if it is too wet, leave the bag open for a day. Seeds or tubers raised in the sphagnum bag will have to be hardened off (see Easing New Plants into the Wider World, page 13) when transplanted.

starting plants in pebbles

Use this easy method for growing root vegetables such as carrots, tubers such as arrowhead, or bulbs such as garlic. Select a water-tight container large enough to hold the vegetable or group of vegetables you wish to plant. Fill two-thirds of the container with rinsed, white pebbles (these are available in garden centers). Place the roots on top of the pebbles and fill in around them with more pebbles. Allow one-third of the plant part to show above the pebbles. Add water to the level of the pebbles and maintain this level at all times.

starting plants in soil

Most root vegetables can be started in potting soil. Buy firm, fresh vegetables and remove all of the leaves from the root, taking care not to nick the flesh. Find a container that is large enough to hold the root (or roots) you are starting and fill it two-thirds full of moist potting soil. Place the roots on top and fill in around them with more potting soil. Allow one-third of the root to show above the soil. Water thoroughly when the surface of the soil feels dry (see Watering Wisdom, page 4).

starting plants from seed

To plant small seeds, fill a container (see page 11 to within an inch of the top with moist potting soil. Then scatter seeds on the surface and cover with more potting soil. Usually, you should cover the seed with twice as much soil as the seed is thick: A ¼-inch seed should be covered with a ½ inch of soil. Press tiny, dustlike seeds into the soil with your fingers. Slip a plastic bag over the seed container and put it in a warm place until the seeds germinate. (Most seeds do not need light to germinate.)

CLEANING SEEDS

The seeds of some fruits and vegetables such as papaya, pomegranate, and bitter melon are surrounded by a fleshy sac called an *aril*. This must be removed before the seeds are sown or stored. (If left on, the rotting aril could attract bugs or fungus.) To do this, take a tablespoon of seeds and scatter them on a double layer of paper towels. Gently flatten the aril. When the seed pops out, move it to a clean towel to dry. Seeds may be sown immediately or dried and stored in an airtight container.

Some seeds, because of their small size or the stickiness of their flesh, are difficult to clean on a paper towel; tamarillo, fig, and guava are examples. These seeds must be cleaned by fermenting. Scoop out the seeds and remove as much flesh as you can. Put the seeds into a small container of water and soak them for a couple of days. The remaining flesh will rise to the top. Drain the seeds and rub on a paper towel. These seeds can be sown immediately or dried and stored in an airtight jar for several months.

The seeds of citrus, cherimoya, and loquat just need a gentle wash when taken from the fruit. Some must be sown immediately; others can be dried and stored in airtight jars.

Containers. Delicatessens are my favorite "pot shops." They have containers of all sizes for soups, sandwiches, salads, and in our case, sphagnum bags and seed flats. My favorite flat is the clear plastic container with a snap lid. The lid ensures humidity for seedlings and can be slowly lifted to harden them off (see Easing New Plants into the Wider World, page 13) as they grow.

Peat pellets. You can also start small seeds in round disks called *peat pellets.* Available at most garden centers, peat pellets are flat, 2-inch round disks filled with compressed peat and surrounded by netting. They combine the function of a pot and potting soil. When the pellets are dry they look like cookies, but if you wet them, they expand into 2-inch-tall pots. Place each pellet in ¼ cup of water and wait five minutes for it to expand. Peat pellets are especially useful for growing plants with tender tap roots, such as papayas and dates.

To sow seeds in the pellets, remove a small amount of peat from the top, insert the seed or seeds, and cover with the peat you removed. Put the sown pellets in a flat or tray that is just big enough to hold several of them. Add water when they seem dry. Cover the flat or tray with a plastic bag to insure humidity and place it in bright light, but not direct sun.

WHEN "COLD" IS A GOOD THING

Seeds from fruits of northern and temperate climates require a cold period before they can germinate. Among seeds that benefit from this cold treatment are chestnuts, almonds, and kiwi. The process of exposing the seeds to cold is called *stratification*, which mimics winter in the plants' original habitats and breaks the seeds' dormancy.

To stratify, fill half a plastic container with moistened peat moss, scatter the seeds on the moss, cover with a plastic bag and place it in the refrigerator. Check weekly to be sure the peat is still moist. After six to eight weeks, remove the container and place it in a warm spot in the house. Keep the plastic bag over it. Expect germination within three weeks.

CARING FOR NEW PLANTS

You must know how best to care for your plants, so that they will flourish. You should know how to provide your tropical plants with heat from the bottom, harden off all of your plants to ease their transition into the outside environment, and transplant to pots once your plants are established.

bottom heat

Many seeds, tubers, and roots, such as dates, papaya, and pomegranate, come from tropical countries. They will sprout faster if they are supplied with bottom heat. Garden centers sell heating mats that can be placed on a surface, such as a tray or water-tight pan to aid germination, as well as mini-greenhouses that come with a heated base. Follow the manufacturer's instructions for using these. You want the soil to be 70°F–80°F. You can also use a food warming tray set on low, but be careful as these can get too hot. The top of a grow light unit gives off just the right amount of heat.

easing new plants into the wider world

As seedlings grow in their container or flat, you will have to remove the plastic bag covering them, but you must do it slowly. This process is called *hardening off*. The air inside the bag is much more humid than the desert-like conditions in most homes, so to ease the transition, punch holes in the bag and leave it on for about a week before taking it off.

transplanting

Once your seedlings have two sets of leaves, they are ready to be transplanted to individual small pots or containers. You can use short plastic cups for containers, but before you plant, you must make drainage holes in these cups. To do this, heat a small skewer in a gas flame or on the heating coil of an electric stove until it is hot, then carefully push it through the bottom of the cup. Make several holes in each cup.

Transplanting small seedlings from a flat is a delicate task. Fill your container to within an inch of the top with moist potting soil. Make a hole in the soil that will be deep enough to contain the roots of your plant. Gently loosen the soil around the seedling and move it out with a spoon. Hold the seedling by a leaf (should you break the stem, the plant will die, but it can always grow another leaf) and gently drop it into the hole. Gently fill in around roots, being careful not to cover the stem with soil.

time to repot?

Keep plants in pots just big enough to let them grow until the roots fill the container. A simple rule of thumb is to use a pot that is 1 inch wider than the width of the crown of the plant, or if it is a tuber, 1 inch wider than the tuber. If pots are too big, the young plant's roots will be surrounded by excess soil and will become waterlogged, which in turn can encourage root diseases. Not all plants are affected by this type of root environment, but to be on the safe side, it's best to gradually increase the plant's soil volume. Plants can stay in small pots for a long time before their growth and size become restricted.

When a plant grows too big for its pot, however, it has to be repotted. When the roots have no place to expand, they go around and around the inside of the pot, virtually strangling the plant. If you find yourself having to water every day, this can be a sign that the plant has outgrown its container.

To see if a plant needs repotting, water it first, then, holding the stem between your fingers, turn the pot upside down. Rap the rim against a hard surface. The whole ball of earth in the pot will slide forward. If the roots completely fill the ball of earth so that no soil can be removed from the surface, it is time to repot.

Use a pot that is roughly an inch larger in diameter than the old one. Place a piece of nylon screening or some porous netting in the bottom of the pot. This will hold the soil in the pot but allow water to run off. Pour an inch of soil mix into the pot and place the plant on top. Fill the area around the plant with fresh soil, then tap the side of the pot to settle the soil around the roots. Press down on the soil around the stem with your fingers. Add more soil, if needed, to bring the soil level to within an inch of the rim of the pot — this leaves plenty of room for watering.

summer camp

The best thing you can do for your plants is to put them outdoors for the summer. It is as close as you can come to providing their natural environment — fresh air, gentle breezes, warm sun, and clean rain water.

Some people fear plants will pick up bugs — quite the contrary. One summer night Milly and I put out a sickly bay plant that was covered with mealy bugs; the next morning it was clean and two very fat ladybugs were lolling on its leaves.

To avoid shock and to create a natural transition from the inside to the outside, put the plants out when the outside daytime temperature is similar to that of the house. Place them in an area that gets just morning or late afternoon sun when you first bring them out; this will help the plants adjust to outdoor light, so that you can subsequently move them into a brighter spot.

There is a big difference between the dull light of the home and the bright summer sun. Your plants will need some protection to prevent scorching; make sure that they receive enough moisture and receive some shade, if appropriate.

I leave the plants outdoors until early October, or when I turn on the heat in the house for the winter. Your plants will be bigger, bushier, and healthier. Although pests often disappear when you take the plants outdoors, they usually return once the plants are brought inside. To prevent pests from getting on other healthy plants in your home, be sure to prune the plants you've had outdoors and treat them for pests before bringing them in. Now is also a good time to check the roots and repot the plants, if necessary.

Dealing with Pests

Here's a rundown of some of the most common pests that you might encounter, along with suggestions on how to deal with them. The best method is prevention. A sterile growing medium; clean pots; well-scrubbed tubers, pits, and seeds; plenty of ventilation; and no overcrowding will usually help you to be pest-free.

aphids

Description. Also known as plant lice, these sap-sucking insects are found in dense colonies on the new growth or flowers of a plant. They come in many colors (black, red, green, yellow, pink, brown, white, for example) and are about the size of the head of a pin.

¹⁄₁₂"/.3cm

Treatment. The best method is to spray them off with an alcohol solution that is one part alcohol to two parts water with a drop of liquid soap. If it is summer, put the plant outdoors; ladybugs will clean the plant overnight.

If you cannot control your insect problem by these methods, the infestation is too bad. I advise tossing the infested plant before the bugs spread to other plants. Planticide is not a crime.

mealybugs

Description. Masses of white, cottony, ⅛-inch tufts found at the leaf axils (spot between the stem and the leaf stalk) and the undersides of the leaves.

⅛"/.4cm

Treatment. Remove these with a cotton swab dipped in the following solution: one part alcohol to two parts water with a drop of liquid soap that acts as a wetting agent. Touch the swab to the fluff; the fluff will dissolve instantly, revealing a small round insect. Brush him off with the tip of the swab. You can also fill a sprayer with the same solution and jet the liquid into hard-to-reach places. Repeat this process every couple of days to make sure you have cleaned the plant.

scale

Description. These hard, brown disks are about twice the size of the head of a pin and are found on the undersides of leaves and along the stems and branches of the plant.

1/16"- ⅛"/.4cm

Treatment. Scales are nasty little sucking insects. Removing them is unpleasant; you must squeeze them hard in order to kill them. I loosen them with a swab soaked in rubbing alcohol and push them on a hard surface. Go over the plant again in a few days. You'll be amazed at how many you missed.

Once the plant is clean, use light horticultural oil (very similar to dormant oil used on outdoor plants) to prevent scale from returning. Follow the instructions on the product and spray the plant completely. I spray twice a year: once in the spring and once in the fall.

sooty mold

Description. A black, oily fungus that forms on the leaves.
Treatment. It washes off easily with soap and water.
Sooty mold is usually a sign of poor air circulation and crowding, so by fixing these two things, you can prevent it from returning.

spider mites

¹⁄₅₀"/.05cm

Description. These nasty little devils are barely visible to the human eye, but you can see their webs on the undersides of leaves.
Treatment. I treat them with a bit of creativity. On a day when temperatures are below 42°F, I spray the infected plants with water, covering all surfaces. Then I put the plant outdoors for a couple of hours. The mites disappear from the plant.

white fly

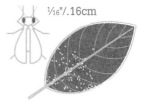

¹⁄₁₆"/.16cm

Description. If you brush past your plant and a small cloud of white flutters up, you have white fly. These are generally found on the undersides of leaves.
Treatment. White flies can spread quickly to other plants. You must isolate the plant and wash it thoroughly with an alcohol solution that is one part alcohol to two parts water with a drop of liquid soap. The life cycle of these bugs is a matter of days. When you think the plant is clean, wash it with plain soap and water each day for several days to destroy all eggs. Adult white flies are attracted to the color yellow; garden centers sell sticky yellow strips that you can put near or in the pot to catch any remaining adults.

CHAPTER 2

plants from common VEGETABLES

Ever since Milly and I started growing roots like beets and turnips indoors, I cannot think of them as just vegetables. They are now houseplants as well, and when I shop for them, I am not only buying tonight's dinner but also preparing a centerpiece for the table.

You'll have many surprises in store when you grow plants from whole vegetables and vegetable seeds. Turnips and radishes bloom. Sweet potatoes have small purple flowers like morning glories. The leaves of the white potato are crinkly, and its flowers come in shades from white to purple. Chickpeas make charming hanging-basket plants. Squash flowers, when pollinated by hand, can bear small squash. One note: All dried legumes, except split peas, will grow for you. Try them all.

Although many of the plants in this chapter last only a few months, they are attractive and should not be missed.

Bean

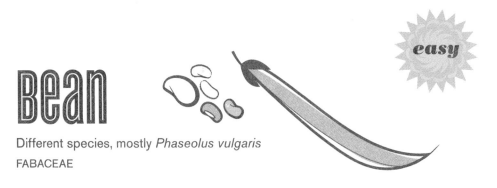

Different species, mostly *Phaseolus vulgaris*
FABACEAE

easy

PLANT TYPE *annual*   **METHOD** *from seed*
GROWTH RATE *quick-growing*   **LIGHT** *bright sun*

WHAT IT LOOKS LIKE

The types of beans classified as "bush beans" generally grow to about
1 foot high. Plants produce pastel-colored flowers.

HOW TO GROW IT

If you are using dried beans, rinse them in a colander and soak them
overnight; if you are using fresh beans, plant immediately. Fill two-thirds of
a 4-inch pot with potting soil, tamping the mix down to settle the soil and
remove large air pockets. Place three beans on the soil about an inch apart
and cover with a ½ inch of soil. Keep the soil constantly damp, not wet,
until the beans sprout, which should be a matter of days.

As the plants grow, snip out the smaller specimens and allow one
good-sized plant to remain and grow. Keep the pot on a sunny windowsill
and water well. If you look at your bean plant at night, you might think it is
drooping. This is nothing to be concerned about, however, as bean leaves
naturally close up at night.

Your bean plant will flower and, because beans self-pollinate, bear edible seed pods in about eight weeks. Pot-grown beans will be smaller than those grown in a farmer's field. If you let the pods mature, you can plant your own home-grown seeds.

ORIGIN

WESTERN HEMISPHERE. When European explorers first arrived in the New World, they found the indigenous people eating hundreds of different kinds of beans. Lima beans, white navy beans, black beans, pinto beans, string beans, and many other kinds were all available in what is now North, South, and Central America. Nearly every region had its own special kind of bean, and soon the explorers spread these plants all around the world.

Beans as Sprouts

Beans are among the easiest and most delicious seeds to sprout. Rich in many vitamins and minerals, sprouts have been used in Asian cooking for centuries. Kidney beans, lima beans, navy beans, pinto beans, soy beans, and mung beans can all be sprouted.

To sprout beans, take ¼ cup of dried beans and rinse them to wash off dust and dirt. Soak them overnight using about four times as much lukewarm water as beans. In the morning, rinse the beans in a strainer and spread them thinly over the bottom of a container large enough so that they can be scattered over the surface without crowding. A flat, watertight container, such as a rimmed tray, is ideal. Lay wet paper towels over the beans, cover with another dish, and set in a warm place. Be sure the paper remains wet. The next day, rinse the beans in a strainer and spread them out on a container again. Moisten more paper towels and cover. Rinse the seeds every day. (Larger beans sprout better if rinsed twice a day.)

Soybean and mung bean sprouts are ready to be used when they are 2 or 3 inches long. They reach this size in four or five days. Mung beans can be eaten raw. Other large beans should be harvested when they are about 1 inch long, which takes about three days. The large beans should be shelled and cooked for a few minutes before they are eaten.

Although it's not a bean, you might want to try sprouting corn in the same way: it's so sweet, you'd think it was pure sugar.

Beet

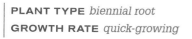

Beta vulgaris
CHENOPODIACEAE

easy

PLANT TYPE *biennial root*	**METHOD** *in soil/in pebbles*
GROWTH RATE *quick-growing*	**LIGHT** *low light*

WHAT IT LOOKS LIKE

Beets have stunning dark green foliage with thick red stems. The leaves reach a length of 6 to 8 inches.

HOW TO GROW IT

Buy only firm, fresh beet roots with tiny new leaves sprouting at the top. Select a soup bowl or serving dish and fill it two-thirds full with moist potting soil. Remove all the foliage from the beets, being careful not to nick the flesh. Place the beets on top of the soil, pressing them in gently and leaving two-thirds of the beet exposed. Fill in around the beets with more moist soil and water well. Beets can also be grown on pebbles (See Starting Plants in Pebbles, page 9.)

Within five days, leaves and stems emerge from the tops of the beets. Once the leaves have emerged, you can use this dish garden as a centerpiece for the table, especially during the winter holidays. The dark red stems and glossy green leaves are a compliment to the season.

The foliage will die down in about two or three weeks, but don't throw the beets out at this point. Beets are biennials, which means it takes two years to go from seed to bloom. The roots you buy in the store formed underground the first year; if you leave them in the ground another year, the plants will bear flowers and seeds. When you plant a beet root in a pot, you "jump the gun" on its natural development, and if you are lucky, a pale-purple flower stalk will shoot up from the root.

ORIGIN

MEDITERRANEAN COASTAL AREA. The ancestor of the beet is a sprawling seaside plant called a *sea beet.* These still grow along the Mediterranean coasts of southern Europe. Sea beets have tough, woody, slender roots not at all like the tender beet root that has been cultivated from it over the course of centuries.

CaRROT

Daucus carota, APIACEAE

PLANT TYPE *biennial root*	**METHOD** *in pebbles*
GROWTH RATE *quick-growing*	**LIGHT** *bright sun*

WHAT IT LOOKS LIKE

Carrots have lovely feathery green leaves.

HOW TO GROW IT

Cut off the top 2 inches of several carrots. Select a bowl or shallow dish and follow the instructions under Starting Plants in Pebbles (page 9). After the green leaves appear, the plants are short-lived (three to six weeks), but since they are so easy to grow, you can have sprouting carrot tops as often as you use carrots in preparing meals.

You can also plant a whole carrot root in soil in a deep flower pot. In six to eight weeks, after leafing out, the plant may send up a stalk with flowers that resemble those of Queen Anne's lace.

ORIGIN

CENTRAL ASIA. The Ancient Greeks believed carrots to be an aphrodisiac. By the first century C.E., the plant was being cultivated for medicinal purposes — as a tonic, as a poultice, and for snakebites.

CHICKPEA

Cicer arietinum, FABACEAE

PLANT TYPE *annual*
GROWTH RATE *quick-growing*

METHOD *from seed*
LIGHT *bright sun*

WHAT IT LOOKS LIKE

Chickpeas, also called garbanzos and ceci bean, have delicate green leaves on long stems and white or reddish blue flowers.

HOW TO GROW IT

Fill two-thirds of a 4-inch pot with moist potting soil. Place three dry chickpeas on top and cover with a ½ inch of soil. Cover container with a plastic sheet or bag to ensure adequate humidity. Seeds germinate within a few days. When sprouts appear, remove the plastic and put the container in a sunny place.

Try this plant in a hanging basket. The plants need full sun, warmth, and lots of water to produce flowers and fruit. Chickpea is short-lived and begins to die after about six months.

ORIGIN

EUROPE AND CENTRAL ASIA. The exact origin of the chickpea is buried in antiquity. The plant grows wild throughout Europe and Central Asia and may well have been one of the staples of early man. Egyptians, Hebrews, and Greeks are known to have grown it, and today chickpeas are cultivated throughout the tropical and subtropical parts of the world.

JeRUSALem ARTICHOKe

Helianthus tuberosus, ASTERACEAE

PLANT TYPE *perennial tuber*
GROWTH RATE *quick-growing*

METHOD *in soil*
LIGHT *low light*

WHAT IT LOOKS LIKE

Round or oblong, with little nubs and smooth, light brown skin, Jerusalem artichokes look like bumpy potatoes. The Jerusalem artichoke is a fast-growing plant that can attain a height of 3 to 5 feet. The plant's leaves, some 3 inches long, are soft and fuzzy green. The flowers look like small yellow sunflowers.

HOW TO GROW IT

Put a whole tuber in a bag of moist peat moss and keep the bag in a warm place. (See The Secret of the Sphagnum Bag, page 8). The tuber germinates rapidly, and within a week, top buds begin to swell and thick roots develop. One tuber can yield as many as 15 stems. When its roots are 3 inches long and the buds clearly swollen, it's time to get the tuber into a pot.

Because the Jerusalem artichoke is an exceptionally large plant, select a pot about 3 inches longer than the tuber is wide. Plant the tuber horizontally in potting soil. Do not cover completely with soil, but allow the buds to show just above the surface. The plant blooms in late August, if placed in a cool southern window or planted outside in the garden. The foliage dies back in a few months, but new tubers will have formed underground to produce new plants.

BEWARE THIS PLANT

I once made the mistake of planting a few Jerusalem artichokes in my country garden in Scituate, Massachusetts. Thirty years later they are still with me and have formed an enormous clump of scraggy 8-foot perennial plants. If you're tempted to plant your Jerusalem artichoke outdoors, beware that it is invasive!

ORIGIN

NORTH AMERICA. The Jerusalem artichoke neither came from Jerusalem nor is it an artichoke. It probably developed from a species of sunflower that is found in the Mississippi Valley. When the French explorer Samuel de Champlain arrived at Cape Cod in 1605, he found the plant being used as food by the Native Americans. Although it did not reach Europe until the early part of the seventeenth century, it is now grown throughout the Northern Hemisphere.

Lentil

Lens culinaris, FABACEAE

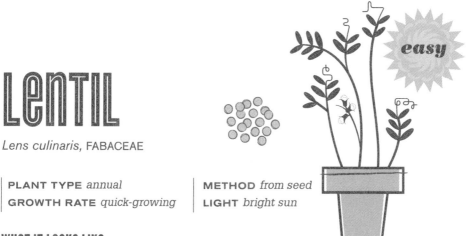

PLANT TYPE *annual*	**METHOD** *from seed*
GROWTH RATE *quick-growing*	**LIGHT** *bright sun*

WHAT IT LOOKS LIKE

A lentil plant is a pretty sight, growing a foot tall, with delicate gray-green leaves and small bluish flowers.

HOW TO GROW IT

Fill a 4-inch pot two-thirds full with moist potting soil. Place a half dozen lentils on the soil and cover with a ¼ inch of soil. Place the pot in a brightly lit window and keep the soil moist. Seeds sprout within a few days. The plant will last a few months.

ORIGIN

ASIA. Lentils have been found in prehistoric sites in Asia and Europe and in Egyptian tombs over 4,000 years old. Egyptians apparently believed that lentils increased mental powers; the Romans believed the opposite. Today lentils are a worldwide staple.

PACKED WITH PROTEIN

Lentils are high in protein and are a staple of a vegetarian diet. Three and one-half ounces of dried lentils contain 26 grams of protein. During World War I, patriotic Americans were encouraged to eat lentils and save meat "for the boys overseas."

ONION, GARLIC, AND SHALLOT

Allium species
ALLIACEAE

PLANT TYPE *perennial bulb*	**METHOD** *in soil/in pebbles*
GROWTH RATE *quick-growing*	**LIGHT** *bright sun*

WHAT IT LOOKS LIKE

The bud inside an *Allium* bulb produces long, bright green leaves. These are all favorite plants to grow. Milly used to grow a delightful exhibit using five types of onions, and I never give a talk without a garlic sprouting in a bonsai dish.

HOW TO GROW IT

Select a bowl or serving dish about 3 to 4 inches high (a Chinese soup bowl does nicely). Onions can be grown on pebbles or in soil (see Starting Plants in Pebbles and Starting Plants in Soil, page 9). Leave the dish in a bright place. Roots will emerge from the bottom of the bulb first, followed by green shoots out of the top. If you use this dish garden as a dining-room centerpiece, your guests can snip off the green leaves and learn the subtle taste differences among the shoots of onion, garlic, and shallots.

You can also produce your own garlic or shallots to use in cooking. Simply break up bulbs into individual cloves and plant them in soil mixture in a container or pot about 1 inch deep and 5 inches apart. Put the pot in a sunny place and fertilize every two weeks. Each clove will produce a whole bulb with many cloves.

ORIGIN

THE ONION FAMILY HAS BEEN KNOWN SINCE THE DAWN OF HISTORY. The Egyptians saw the onion as a model of the universe because they thought the spheres of hell, earth, and heaven were also in concentric rings. Garlic has always been thought to be a good preventive against various illnesses, and some claim it is valuable as an aid to digestion, in reducing high blood pressure, and relieving bronchitis. Onions contain substances that act as antiseptics and anti-inflammatories.

Pea

Pisum sativum, FABACEAE

PLANT TYPE *annual bush/vine*	**METHOD** *from seed*
GROWTH RATE *quick-growing*	**LIGHT** *bright light*

WHAT IT LOOKS LIKE

Available as either bush or vine, peas have small, rounded green leaves and lovely white flowers. They are available fresh in spring and early summer in most supermarkets.

HOW TO GROW IT

Open a fresh pea pod and remove the seeds, or use dried peas that have been soaked overnight. Fill a 4-inch pot two-thirds full with moist potting soil. Place three peas on the surface and cover with an inch of soil. Place the pot in a sunny window that doesn't get too hot; water when the soil dries out and apply liquid fertilizer every two weeks. Peas sprout in a week; vine types climb by means of tendrils and need to be supported with a trellis. Pea flowers are self-pollinating, so the plant will bear fruit if grown in a cool, sunny place.

ORIGIN

EUROPE. Peas have been found in 5,000-year-old dwellings in the lake region of Switzerland. From there they spread southward to Sumer (today the part of Iraq near the Persian Gulf) and then to Egypt.

Fresh peas were the rage in Europe about the time that Catherine de Medici became queen of France in 1547. In 1669, the memoirist and member of the French court Madame de Maintenon described the passion for peas as a kind of madness: "The anxiety to eat them, the pleasure of having eaten them, and the desire to eat them again, are the three great matters which have been discussed by our princes for four days past."

The pea's popularity rapidly spread to the English court and to the American colonies. Today peas are cultivated in all countries with a temperate climate.

POTATO

Solanum tuberosum

SOLANACEAE

easy

PLANT TYPE *annual tuber*	**METHOD** *in soil*
GROWTH RATE *slow-growing*	**LIGHT** *bright sun*

WHAT IT LOOKS LIKE

A potato plant grows 2 to 3 feet tall and produces pretty purple flowers that resemble tomato blossoms. All parts of the potato plant except the tuber itself are poisonous.

ORIGIN — **SOUTH AMERICA.** The potato was brought from South America to Europe by Spanish sailing ships during the sixteenth century and was subsequently introduced to North America by European settlers during the early seventeenth century.

HOW TO GROW IT

Pick a small potato with buds already starting to sprout. Fill one-third of a 6-inch pot with moist potting soil and put the potato on the soil. Cover with an inch of soil. Keep the plant in bright sun and water when dry. Instead of using a whole potato, you can also cut a slice that includes an eye (sprout). Dry the slice on the kitchen counter overnight to help callus (harden) the cut surface. Plant it in a pot large enough to hold the slice, making sure the eye is on the soil surface.

No matter which method you use, small potatoes will form underground. You can enjoy your minuscule crop in the pot or, if you have a garden, transplant the potato plants into the soil. You will have a small crop at the end of the summer.

RaDISH

Raphanus sativus, BRASSICACEAE

PLANT TYPE *annual*	**METHOD** *in soil/in pebbles*
GROWTH RATE *quick-growing*	**LIGHT** *bright light*

WHaT IT LOOKS LIKe

The radish has small, crinkly green leaves that contrast beautifully with its round red roots. This fast-growing plant may send up a flower stalk, and if the plants bloom, your dish garden is a sight to behold.

ORIGIN

CHINA. Radishes are mentioned frequently in ancient writings. They were cultivated in Egypt at the time of the Pharaohs. Egyptian Pharaohs allegedly made radishes part of the daily diet of the slaves who built the pyramids and Ancient Greeks made offerings of radishes to Apollo on gold plates (while turnips were offered on lead and beets on silver).

In medieval Europe, the radish was considered to have magical and medicinal properties. It was used to detect witches, cure madness, and exorcize demons. More mundanely, radishes were thought to cure headaches, shingles, eye aches, and joint pains, and to remove warts and black-and-blue marks.

HOW TO GROW IT

Radishes can be grown on pebbles or potted in soil. (See Starting Plants in Pebbles and Starting Plants in Soil, page 9.) Radish dish gardens last only a few weeks, but because they are so easy to grow, you can always start a new one.

SUMMER SQUASH

Cucurbita pepo, CUCURBITACEAE

PLANT TYPE *annual*	**METHOD** *from seed*
GROWTH RATE *quick-growing*	**LIGHT** *bright light*

WHAT IT LOOKS LIKE

Outdoors, summer squash develops strong, spreading vines. Grown indoors, the plant is smaller, with heart-shaped leaves that trail over the pot. The large yellow flowers that appear in three to six weeks are edible.

HOW TO GROW IT

Remove the seeds from the squash and scrub off excess pulp. Plant the seeds immediately or dry them completely and store for later use. Squash are large vining plants that can suffer from transplant shock, so start them in peat pellets. Place the pellets on a tray, then slip a plastic bag over the container to maintain humidity. The seeds germinate in less than a week.

When the seedlings show, remove the plastic bag and put the container in a sunny window. When roots protrude through the pellets, it is time to transplant. For each pellet, fill a 6-inch pot one-third full with moist potting soil, place a pellet on the soil, and fill in around it, barely covering it with soil. Keep the pots in a sunny place, water regularly, and fertilize every week. Flowers appear after the leaves. Squash may also be sown directly into a 6-inch hanging basket.

There are two kinds of flowers: male and female. The former has only stamens, which contain the pollen; the latter has a green bulge, which is the ovary, behind the petals. Outdoors, bees transfer the pollen from the male flowers to the female. Indoors, you will not have any fruit unless you do the pollinating yourself. Take a small paintbrush and touch it to the pollen of a male flower, then touch the brush to the center of the female flower. Within a week, the fruit should begin to develop.

ORIGIN NORTH AND SOUTH AMERICA. When the first explorers came to the New World, they found the indigenous people growing different kinds of squash. The name comes from the Narragansett word *askutasquash*.

SWEET POTATO

Ipomoea batatas, CONVOLVULACEAE

PLANT TYPE *annual tuber*	**METHOD** *in water*
GROWTH RATE *quick-growing*	**LIGHT** *bright light*

WHAT IT LOOKS LIKE

The sweet potato is a vine that can cover a window in a short time.
Its heart-shaped leaves resemble those of a morning glory, except the
sweet potato leaves have lovely purple veins. The potato plant will last
for months. (In the right pot this humble plant can look like a stylish
caudiciform, which is a succulent treasured for its swollen trunk.)

HOW TO GROW IT

Because many sweet potatoes have been dried in kilns or treated to keep
them from sprouting, you need to take some care in finding the right ones
to plant. Look for a sweet potato that has some sign of life, such as some
roots or little purple buds. Stick three toothpicks or bamboo skewers into
the sides of the sweet potato about one-third of the way down from the
top (the top is rounder in shape than the bottom). Set the potato in a tall,
opaque jar of water with the toothpicks resting on the rim. Add water as it
evaporates. A tablespoon of activated charcoal will keep the water sweet.
(See Starting Plants in Water, page 7.) Set the jar on a windowsill in bright
light, in a warm place.

When the jar is full of roots you can transplant the potato to a pot large enough to hold the whole plant. Leave one-third of the potato above the soil. You will see a stem and leaf buds first, followed by flowers.

DOUBLE THE PLEASURE

Here is a wonderful experiment to try: A friend asked if she could clip several of my sweet potato stems. She laid them down horizontally in a large planter and tacked the vines down with hair pins. In a matter of weeks, new plants sprouted along the stems. Her planter is full of individual plants that sprouted from the stems and these in turn developed many small sweet potatoes.

ORIGIN

SOUTH AND CENTRAL AMERICA. When Columbus came to what are now the Americas, he found many varieties of sweet potato growing. Today there are still many grown in tropical and subtropical countries throughout the world.

TURNIP

Brassica rapa, BRASSICACEAE

PLANT TYPE *biennial root*	**METHOD** *in soil/in pebbles*
GROWTH RATE *quick-growing*	**LIGHT** *bright sun*

WHAT IT LOOKS LIKE

Like carrots and beets, the turnip is a biennial. Planted indoors, it will produce a rosette of rough, curly green leaves. If they appear, flowers are small and yellow and resemble those of the mustard seed.

HOW TO GROW IT

Turnips may be grown in pebbles or soil. (See Starting Plants in Pebbles and Starting Plants in Soil, page 9.) Cut off the bottom half of one large turnip and place the top half, cut side down, on the pebbles or soil. Add more pebbles or soil to hold the turnip in place. Add water to the level of the pebbles and maintain this water level always. If using soil, keep it moist. Place the bowl in bright light. Green leaves appear first, sometimes followed by flowers.

ORIGIN

RUSSIA, SIBERIA, AND THE SCANDINAVIAN PENINSULA. Turnips have been cultivated since ancient times. Greek writings describe 100-pound turnips. The small white turnips we buy today were probably developed by the Dutch.

CHAPTER 3

plants from FRUITS & NUTS

The part of a plant that contains its seeds is technically the fruit. This means that the avocado is a fruit, and so is a peanut or an almond. The seeds you find within fresh fruits are the best you can buy to start your own plants. They haven't been treated, dried, and stored before arriving in the market. Many people are familiar with the idea of taking an avocado pit and growing a new plant from it, but the seeds of such fruits as dates, grapefruit, and mangos can also be grown into attractive houseplants. The date becomes a palm tree. Citrus seeds grow into beautiful small trees with shiny green leaves. The pineapple makes an exotic plant, with long, sword-shaped leaves.

Once you start growing these wonderful plants, you will think twice before tossing away a pineapple top or the seeds of any other fruit that you might have eaten for lunch. Wonderful gardening and adventurous eating await you!

ALMOND

Prunus amygdalus
ROSACEAE

PLANT TYPE *deciduous tree*	**METHOD** *from seed*
GROWTH RATE *quick-growing*	**LIGHT** *low light*

WHAT IT LOOKS LIKE

An almond tree grown from a nut makes a most unusual houseplant. The leaves of the plant are long and pointed. In nature, the five-petaled blooms are a beautiful white and pink.

HOW TO GROW IT

The edible part of the almond is the pit of the almond fruit, which looks like a dried peach. When the fruit falls from the tree, the fibrous outer husk splits, and the nuts can be removed from the husks.

Almonds do not germinate readily unless they are stratified (see When "Cold" Is a Good Thing, page 12). To accomplish this, put almonds, either shelled or unshelled, in a bag of moist peat moss, and place the bag in the refrigerator for six to eight weeks. Remove and then extract the seeds (better known as the nuts) from the bag. (If the almonds are not already shelled, you'll need to remove them from their shells.) Plant one seed per peat pellet (see Starting Plants from Seed, page 10).

When roots fill the pellets, transplant each pellet to a 4-inch pot. Fill one-third of the pot with moist potting soil, place the pellet on the soil, and add enough soil to barely cover it.

At this point, the almond grows with spectacular speed; it seems to jump by inches and becomes leggy very quickly. To keep the young tree shapely and encourage branching, cut back the main stem.

ORIGIN

NORTH AFRICA AND ASIA. Almonds were enjoyed by both the ancient Hebrews and the seafaring Phoenicians. They are now grown in almost every country with a temperate climate.

easy

AVOCADO

Persea species, LAURACEAE

PLANT TYPE *evergreen tree*	**METHOD** *from seed*
GROWTH RATE *quick-growing*	**LIGHT** *bright light*

WHAT IT LOOKS LIKE

As avocado plants grow, they develop small clusters of leaves around 6-inch stems, which grow taller and taller without producing any branches. The avocado can become one of the most beautiful plants in your home. At one time Milly had a 36-inch barrel into which she had set ten avocados in varying stages of development. It formed a cool, refreshing grove at the end of the living room.

HOW TO GROW IT

When Milly and I first experimented with growing avocados, there were two main types. The larger, grown in Florida, had shiny, dark green skins and a large pit that could be 2 inches across. This particular pit germinated quite readily — in fact, you often found it with roots already started. Avocados from California were smaller, some with purple, nubby skin; others smooth and green. The pit found in the latter avocados was also smaller and more difficult to germinate. Within these two groups there were over 400 hybrids.

Today, commercial selections are limited to the Haas avocado, a hybrid of the California type of fruit, and the large Florida avocado (a.k.a. alligator pear). The Haas has a rich, buttery texture and pleasant nutty flavor.

After some experimentation, we found that the sphagnum bag method was easier and more reliable than the more common practice of puncturing the avocado seed and suspending it in a glass of water. (See The Secret of the Sphagnum Bag, page 8.) Germination time varies with each pit, but the average time is a few weeks.

When the roots are 3 to 4 inches long, transfer the avocado to a pot 1 inch larger than the pit. Fill the pot one-third full with potting soil. Gently place the pit on the soil and fill in enough soil around it so that half the pit is exposed at the top. Place the pot in a warm, bright spot (avocados do not require direct sunlight). Once established, avocados grow quite rampantly.

Keep the soil moist, but not soggy, at all times. During their natural resting period from October to January, avocados need less water. As soon as the days lengthen, new leaves will appear and you should give them more water.

ORIGIN

CENTRAL AND SOUTH AMERICA AND THE WEST INDIES

TO PINCH OR NOT TO PINCH?

To encourage branching, the usual technique is to cut the single avocado stem back to within 3 inches of the pit. Each time the stem is cut back, however, it sprouts a branch that takes over the lead, leaving you with not only another unbranching stem but also a stump where the original stem was cut off. If you do this enough times, your plant will begin to look like a hat rack. Let the avocado go its own way until, about a year later, it starts to branch naturally. At this time you can trim the side branches to make the plant more shapely.

CAROB

Caesalpinioideae, FABACEAE

PLANT TYPE *evergreen shrub/tree*	**METHOD** *from seed*
GROWTH RATE *slow-growing*	**LIGHT** *bright light*

WHAT IT LOOKS LIKE

The pods of the carob (also known as St. John's-bread) look something like large lima bean pods that have turned brown. Inside are hard, shiny seeds. The plant's oval leaves change from shiny, pink-bronze to dark, gray-green when mature. Carob is a slow-growing, stately tree that flourishes in an arid climate. The pods are available year-round in Middle Eastern markets.

HOW TO GROW IT

Remove the seeds from the pod. Nick each seed with a sharp-edged file or a piece of sandpaper, and soak them for one or two days. When the seeds swell, they are ready to plant.

Start in moistened peat pellets. (See Starting Plants from Seed, page 10.) Plant at least three seeds in each. Place the pellets on a tray, slip a plastic bag over the tray, and put it where it will have bottom heat. Water the pellets regularly. The seeds should sprout within a week. When the seedlings show, remove the plastic bag and put the tray in a sunny window.

Transplant seedlings when they are 6 inches tall. Fill 4-inch pots one-third full with moist potting soil. Place a pellet on the soil, fill in around it, and barely cover it with more soil. Place the pots in a bright, sunny window, and keep the soil moist but not soggy. Repot when needed.

Time to Taste

Although carob in the past served as food for human consumption only in times of famine, today carob is sometimes used as a substitute for chocolate. The pods have a mochalike taste and their gummy texture is rather pleasant.

 ORIGIN

MEDITERRANEAN REGION. The dried pods of carob have been found in the ruins of Pompeii. When John the Baptist wandered in the desert, the "wild honey" he was said to have eaten may have been the pulp of these pods. The uniform seeds are supposed to have been used in ancient times by goldsmiths to verify the carat weight of gold.

Chinese Star Apple

Averrhoa camrambola, OXALIDACEAE

PLANT TYPE *evergreen tree*
GROWTH RATE *slow-growing*

METHOD *from seed*
LIGHT *bright light*

WHAT IT LOOKS LIKE

Also known as the star apple or carambola, the Chinese star apple is a stunning addition to any fruit-bowl display. It is ovoid and golden-yellow, with several prominent ribs. When

ORIGIN **EAST INDIES AND CHINA**

you make a horizontal slice of the fruit, the pieces are star-shaped. The leaves of the plant have seven to eleven heart-shaped leaflets, which give the plant a feathery appearance similar to the mimosa tree. At night the leaves close up. This is a truly graceful and charming plant. The fruit is available from the fall to the early winter in specialty food stores and some supermarkets.

HOW TO GROW IT

Not all Chinese star apples have seeds. The fruit is quite translucent and, if you hold it up to the light, you can see the shadow of the seeds, which are deep within the fruit. Carefully remove the seeds and plant them in peat pellets. (See Starting Plants from Seed, page 10.) The seeds germinate within three weeks. When the first set of leaves emerges, remove the plastic bag covering them, and place the seedlings in a bright draft-free window.

When roots fill the pellets or the seedlings are 3 to 4 inches tall, it is time to transplant the seedlings. For each pellet, fill a 4-inch pot one-third full with moist potting soil. Place the pellet on the soil and fill in around it, just barely covering it. Return the pots to a bright, draft-free window. The Chinese star apple grows slowly, about a foot a year, and will not bear fruit indoors.

Time to Taste

In general these fruits make a wonderful addition to any fruit cup or salad, but they vary greatly in quality. At their best, they are like a cross between a sweet grapefruit and an orange. At their worst, they are sour and full of tannic acid. To improve your chances of selecting a sweet one, smell the fruit. If it has a sweet aroma, chances are that it will be sweet. Chinese star apples can be eaten plain or combined with avocado in a salad. Sour varieties can be used to make jams and jellies.

FRUITING CITRUS

Most of the citrus fruits we buy in supermarkets are taken from hybrid trees, developed by crossbreeding varieties for larger, sweeter fruits by taking cuttings from parent trees. Plants grown from seed from these hybrid trees probably themselves will not fruit, and if they do, they may not necessarily bear the same fruit as the hybrids'. On the other hand, some citruses are not crossbreeds, but rather come directly from the species, which means they have the same DNA in their seed as the tree that bore them. The plant will fruit and flower in the home, and the flowers are intensely fragrant. These fruits are quite hard to find. Here are a few to look for:

MEIWA KUMQUAT *(Citrus crassifolia).* This round, 1½-inch fruit with edible skin is available in choice Asian markets in winter. A friend had over 20 fruits on her 3-foot tree in 5 years.

MEYER LEMON *(Citrus × meyeri).* This smooth-skinned, sweet-tasting lemon is available in specialty markets and some supermarkets in winter. Grown from seed, it may bloom in its fourth year.

PONDEROSA LEMON *(Citrus limon* 'Ponderosa').* This is a large, bumpy-skinned lemon that can weigh up to 4 pounds. It is usually propagated by cuttings but bears true from seed. The fruit takes almost a year to ripen. It is seen occasionally in specialty markets.

KAFFIR LIME *(Citrus × hystrix).* This is a 4- to 5-inch, pale-colored lime with a nubby skin. Its leaves, which have a musty odor when crushed, are used in Thai and Indian dishes. Available in fall in Asian markets. I have been waiting for three years for mine to bloom.

CITRUS

[GRAPEFRUIT, KUMQUAT, LEMON, ORANGE, TANGERINE]

Citrus species, RUTACEAE

PLANT TYPE *evergreen tree/shrub*
GROWTH RATE *slow-growing*

METHOD *from seed*
LIGHT *bright sun*

WHAT IT LOOKS LIKE

Outdoors, citrus trees may grow as high as 25 feet. Indoors, however, a plant can reach 10 feet high. Actually, the height depends on the size of the pot and the amount of fertilizing you do. Citrus trees are slow growers — about a foot a year. They branch naturally and, with their dark, glossy leaves, make beautiful houseplants. With enough time and sun, flowers may appear.

HOW TO GROW IT

Select ripe fruit, extract the seeds, give them a rinse, and plant them immediately in peat pellets, one seed to each pellet. (See Starting Plants from Seed, page 10), With your fingers, remove enough peat to place each seed in the soil and cover it

ORIGIN INDIA, CHINA, INDOCHINA, AND BURMA

with the peat you remove. Keep the pellets in a tray to which you can add water so that you can moisten them regularly. Slip a plastic bag over the tray to maintain humidity. The seeds should sprout in two to three weeks. When the seedlings show, remove the plastic bag and put the tray in a sunny window.

As soon as roots fill the pellets, transplant the citrus seedlings to 4-inch pots filled one-third full with moist potting soil to which a pinch of lime or broken eggshell has been added. Place a pellet in each pot and barely cover it with soil. Place the pots in the sunniest spot you have available.

Date

Phoenix dactylifera, ARECACEAE

PLANT TYPE *tree*
GROWTH RATE *slow-growing*

METHOD *from seed*
LIGHT *low light*

WHAT IT LOOKS LIKE

Dates have long, linear leaves.

HOW TO GROW IT

The best way to start dates is to use the light golden-brown dates that have been cured in the sun rather than in kilns. You'll see them advertised as "unpasteurized," "nonsulfured," "natural," or "imported." Select fresh dates in late October and early November when they are available in Asian and Middle Eastern markets. These germinate very quickly.

Remove seeds from the fruit and start the seeds in peat pellets. (See Starting Plants from Seed, page 10.) Insert the seeds, making sure they are well-covered. Place the pellets on a tray, and slide a plastic bag over the tray; give them a high bottom heat of 80°F. Frequently the first sign of growth is a large taproot protruding from the bottom of the pellet. Within three to six weeks a small linear leaf will appear; it is time to transplant.

Using 4-inch pots filled with 2 inches of moist potting soil, place a pellet in each pot. Fill in around it with more soil and barely cover it.

Palms grow slowly, but they require relatively little attention. Contrary to what you might imagine, they do not need full sunlight and are even likely to scorch with too much sun. They must be watered whenever the top soil seems dry, as they do require a considerable amount of water. While progress may be slow at first, this is a plant you can pass on to your grandchildren. Known for their longevity, it was said of them, "They still bring forth fruit in old age, they are ever full of sap and green" (Psalms 92).

PATIENCE PAYS

Palms are very slow growers, and the date palm is no exception. After sitting around looking at one linear leaf for a year, only to be rewarded with two linear leaves the next, Milly and I became discouraged. At the price of New York City real estate, these were turning into very expensive and not very attractive plants. Luckily, we were given a hint from a kitchen gardener in Washington, D.C., who had an absolutely magnificent six-year-old date palm. She said she starts all her dates in the soil at the base of other large plants and just lets them stay there until they are attractive enough to warrant pots of their own.

ORIGIN

NORTH AFRICA AND ARABIA. The date palm has been cultivated for over 4,000 years. In the biblical story of John the Baptist's trek through the wilderness, four varieties are described. Today the date is still an important staple in Middle Eastern diets.

Feijoa

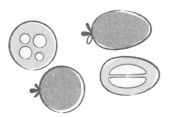

Feijoa sellowiana, MYRTACEAE

PLANT TYPE *evergreen shrub*
GROWTH RATE *quick-growing*

METHOD *from seed*
LIGHT *bright sun*

WHAT IT LOOKS LIKE

Feijoas, also known as pineapple guavas, have ¾- to 3-inch long, oval,
gray-green, leathery-skinned fruits. Each fruit has a distinctive calyx (the
outermost whorl of the flower) at its tip. Within the creamy flesh, there are
dozens of tiny edible seeds.

In nature, feijoa is a bushy evergreen shrub that can grow 15 feet tall
and wide. In the warmer regions of the United States, it is used as a hedge
plant. The leaves are oval, leathery dark green, with a silver underside;
flowers are bright red. Feijoa should not be confused with its more tropical
cousins, the tropical guava (*Psidium guajava*) and the strawberry guava
(*Psidium cattleianum*); they are in the same botanic family (Myrtaceae),
but thrive under different conditions. (See pages 120 and 118.) Feijoas are
available September through November in specialty food stores.

HOW TO GROW IT

The tiny seeds of the feijoa are best cleaned by fermenting. Scoop out a
tablespoon of flesh and seeds from the fruit, and put it in a small container
of water. Let it sit for two or three days. Once the seeds have dropped to

the bottom of the container, pour off the water and flesh, and then dry the seeds on a paper towel. The seeds can be sown immediately or stored in an airtight jar. Stored seed is viable for months.

Sow the feijoa seeds in a container filled with moist potting soil. Scatter the seeds on top of the soil and cover with more soil. Cover the container with plastic to retain humidity and place in a warm, bright spot in the house. The seeds should germinate in two or three weeks. When the seedlings have two sets of leaves, they can be transplanted to small individual pots. You can put established plants in the garden for "summer camp." Otherwise, enjoy indoors.

Here's a trick for getting feijoa to flower. Because the plants need a cooling period of a month at about 40°F, put your plant in your refrigerator, if your fridge is large enough.

ORIGIN   SOUTH AMERICA

Time To Taste

The fruits have a pleasant, sweet taste — pineapple and strawberry combined. They can be eaten fresh or made into preserves. Should your feijoa actually flower, the flowers are also delicious.

FIG

Ficus carica, MORACEAE

PLANT TYPE *deciduous tree*	**METHOD** *from seed*
GROWTH RATE *quick-growing*	**LIGHT** *bright sun*

WHAT IT LOOKS LIKE

Fig trees have large, deeply lobed, exotic-looking leaves that contrast with their somewhat brown, angular stem. They make large indoor plants. Nothing can rival the taste of your own home-grown fig!

HOW TO GROW IT

Buy Smyrna figs, available year-round, or calimyrna figs, available in the fall, from speciality food stores and many large supermarkets. (The seeds of these types of figs are fertile and can grow into new plants, while the seeds of the common fig have no embryos and will not grow.) Remove the pulp containing the fig's seeds, and put it in a small bowl of water. With your fingers, separate as much pulp as possible from the seed, then pour off the water and add more clean water. By the next morning most of the remaining pulp will have dissolved, and the tiny seeds will be at the bottom of the bowl. Pour off the water carefully to retain the seeds.

To plant these seeds, fill a container half full with potting soil, and using a spoon, pick up a few seeds at a time and press them into the mix. Slip a plastic bag over the dish and set it in a warm place. When the fig

ORIGIN **NEAR EAST AND NORTH AFRICA**

seedlings are 4 inches high, select the best ones to grow into large-size plants.

To remove a seedling from the dish, gently loosen the soil underneath it with a pencil and lift it out by the leaves. For each seedling, fill a 4-inch pot with moist potting soil and, using the pencil, make a hole deep enough to receive the roots. Cover the roots, but not the stem, with soil. Water well and place the pot in a sunny window. The fig plants will grow fairly rapidly.

You can transfer fig plants to the garden for the summer, but the plants are deciduous, and as soon as they drop their leaves, it is time to give them a good watering and put them in an unheated garage or basement (or other similar location that will drop to no lower than 15°F) for the winter.

KIWI

Actinidia sinensis, ACTINIDIACEAE

PLANT TYPE *deciduous vine*
GROWTH RATE *quick-growing*

METHOD *from seed*
LIGHT *bright sun*

WHAT IT LOOKS LIKE

With a shape like that of a large gooseberry, the kiwi is brown and hairy, with an almost woody texture to its thin skin; the flesh is a beautiful translucent green. In nature, the kiwi is a deciduous vine attaining a length of 25 feet. Indoors, its size is easily controlled by judicious pruning and by limiting the size of the pot. It is a beautiful plant, with soft, fuzzy, pale green leaves.

HOW TO GROW IT

When you slice the fruit, you'll notice hundreds of tiny black seeds. Scoop out a few and remove all traces of flesh by rolling them on a paper towel with your fingers.

Fill a small plastic container with moist peat moss and scatter the seeds on the surface. Cover lightly with more moist peat. Slip a plastic bag over the container and put the container in the refrigerator, leaving it there for four to six weeks. (See When "Cold" Is a Good Thing, page 12.)

When you remove the seeds from their mock winter, put the container in a warm spot. The seedlings should sprout shortly thereafter. When they do, remove the plastic bag and put the container in a bright window.

When the kiwi seedlings are 2 inches high, transplant them. Gently loosen the soil under each seedling with a pencil and lift the young plant out by the leaves. Fill a 4-inch pot with moist potting soil. Use the pencil to make a hole deep enough to receive the roots, and cover about an inch of the stem with soil. Water well and place the pot in a bright window.

Young seedlings should be staked, and older plants should be given supports on which to twine. Attach the plant to its support with plant ties. Kiwis need careful care and pruning to bring them to fruit, but they are quite hardy and grow outside as far north as New York City.

Time to Taste

The kiwi is a delicious breakfast or dessert fruit. Its flavor is reminiscent of strawberries and watermelon. Try it in a fruit compote as well.

ORIGIN

CHINA. Most kiwis found in markets today are grown in New Zealand and California. For some unknown reason, the fruit has the same name as the flightless kiwi bird of New Zealand.

Mango

Mangifera indica, ANACARDIACEAE

PLANT TYPE *evergreen tree*	**METHOD** *from seed*
GROWTH RATE *slow-growing*	**LIGHT** *low light*

WHAT IT LOOKS LIKE

The mango has been described as the "king of fruits" and the "apple of the tropics," as well as "a ball of tow, soaked in turpentine and molasses, and you have to eat it in the bathtub." As these quotations indicate, there are many varieties of diverse quality. Some mangoes are bright yellow and no larger than a peach, while others are bright green, tinged with red, and can weigh as much as 4 pounds. The most common are oval in shape with waxy, thick skins. When properly ripe, the flesh, which is orange and creamy, yields to the touch, and the fruit gives off a sweet perfume. Poor-quality mangoes have a slight odor of turpentine and are very fibrous, but their pits create good house plants.

The plant's new leaves are an intense red, as is the new trunk. As the leaves mature, they go from red to pink to copper and finally to a dark glossy green.

HOW TO GROW IT

Within the mango, you'll find a large, hairy husk that must be scrubbed so that it can be handled easily. At best, this is a very messy business.

Scraping with a serrated steak knife speeds up the process, but you still need a lot of paper towels and running water. Having cleaned the mango husk, let it dry out overnight.

The next day, to get to the seed (which looks like a large cashew nut) clip off a tiny piece of the husk where there is a slight indentation around the narrow edge of the husk. Then, insert the point of a small knife and work it back and forth until you can grasp the edges of the husk and pry it apart. Care should be taken at all times to avoid hurting the seed inside the husk. You can also try simply cleaning the husk and planting the seed still in it. A friend who doesn't want to put up with all the mess of drying and prying swears by this method.

Mango seeds may be germinated in several ways. My preferred method of germination is to use the sphagnum bag. (See The Secret of the Sphagnum Bag, page 8.) Seeds treated this way develop enormous roots in two to three weeks. Using a 6-inch pot half filled with a moist potting soil, place the sprouted seed on the soil. You will have no trouble deciding which end is down, because the roots and shoots will have formed by the time you plant. Fill in around the seed and cover it with a ¼ inch of soil. Tent the seedling with plastic, to ensure humidity. Gradually remove the plastic over several days, to allow the plant to adjust to the dry conditions of the home. In the early stages of growth, the seedlings should be sheltered from direct sun. Either place among other larger plants or grow them in fluorescent light units.

Time to Taste

Mangos are among the most delicious of all the tropical fruits, but eating one isn't easy. Here is a simple preparation method: Cut two thick, vertical slices of mango, one on either side of the seed, taking care to avoid the seed in the center. Score the flesh with cross hatching (as you would to prepare a ham), then fold back the skin. Small, easily bitten pieces of mango pop up. Pull off the peel in the center slice and chew around the seed. *Warning:* Mangoes are in the Anacardiaceae family, as is poison ivy. Some people are allergic to its skin. This is, however, a rare condition.

ORIGIN

INDIA AND SOUTHEAST ASIA. The mango is now cultivated throughout all tropical regions of the world.

Papaya

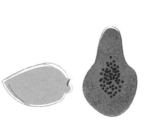

Carica papaya, CARICACEAE

PLANT TYPE *perennial*	**METHOD** *from seed*
GROWTH RATE *slow-growing*	**LIGHT** *bright sun*

WHAT IT LOOKS LIKE

A large pear-shaped fruit, 8 to 10 inches long, the papaya is usually sold green, but it turns yellow when ripe. To ripen, keep in a warm, dark part of the kitchen. At its best, the papaya is a fast-growing, single-stemmed plant that grows to the size of a small tree. In the tropics, papayas can reach a height of 10 feet in 10 months and bear their first crop. Indoors, growth is slower and there will be no fruit. Papayas are dioecious, which means that they require both male and female plants to bear fruit. Although there is no way to tell the sex of your seedlings, however, their deeply lobed, maplelike leaves add an exotic touch to any plant collection. The solo papaya is self-pollinating, and it is possible for it to produce flowers and fruit indoors. The fruit is slow to ripen in a northern climate, but once it does, the taste is terrific.

HOW TO GROW IT

When you slice the papaya, you will see enough seeds to start a plantation. The dark brown seeds are each surrounded by a gelatinous sac called the *aril.* Gently squeeze the nubby, brown seeds onto a paper towel; they look just like peppercorns. You can dry the seeds and store them in an airtight jar.

Plant a few seeds in moistened peat pellets and place in a tray. (See Starting Plants from Seed, page 10.) Slip a plastic bag over the tray and place it over bottom heat. The seeds will germinate within two weeks; at this time remove the plastic bag and put the tray in a bright, but not too sunny, location. Papaya seedlings sometimes suffer from sudden wilt, which is caused by a fungus. If this happens, the safest thing to do is throw them out and buy another papaya.

When the seedlings are a few inches high, pinch out all but the sturdiest plant from each pellet. Transplant to individual 4-inch pots. From this point on, the plants need a lot of water and fertilizer and should be kept in a sunny, warm window. High humidity helps a great deal; a draft does not.

Time to Taste

Papaya is delicious eaten raw, made into papaya juice, or used in chutneys. Just remember that these seeds look a lot like peppercorns. A few years back, I made steak au poivre by cracking some peppercorns and pushing them into the meat before broiling. The only problem was that my "peppercorns" were papaya seeds: we could eat that steak with a spoon. Mark your jars of stored seeds!

CENTRAL AMERICA. Indigenous people have long used papayas to cure indigestion and to tenderize their meat. The active substance in the fruit is papain, an enzyme, which today is the most important ingredient in commercial meat tenderizers.

PEANUT

Arachis hypogaea
FABACEAE

PLANT TYPE *annual*	**METHOD** *from seed*
GROWTH RATE *quick-growing*	**LIGHT** *bright sun*

WHAT IT LOOKS LIKE

The peanut is a pretty plant with compound, oval leaves; it grows to a height of 1 to 2 feet. At night, the leaves fold up into a "sleeping" position, which children find especially interesting. The yellow flowers look like small peas.

HOW TO GROW IT

Be sure to get fresh, unroasted peanuts. These are available in Asian markets and other specialty food markets. Remove the shells, and plant four peanuts in moist potting soil in a 6-inch pot. Cover the peanuts with about an inch of soil. After the plants have germinated and grown to a height of about 4 inches, remove all but the sturdiest plant. Place the pot in a sunny location. Wait until the plant flowers. After it has pollinated itself and its petals have fallen off, the ovary will swell and the plant will start to grow down. It then will push into the earth and eventually a peanut containing two seeds will emerge. If you plant your peanuts close to the outer edge of a clear plastic pot, you'll be able to watch this unusual process.

If you have a garden, start several peanut plants indoors in March in small individual pots. (Low plastic cups are excellent for this, but be sure to make a drainage hole in the bottom of each cup.) When the outdoor temperature levels off at 55°F at night, transplant the peanuts to the garden. You should have a small crop by Columbus Day, or when the foliage begins to yellow.

ORIGIN

SOUTH AMERICA. The peanut plant has traveled all over the world from its first home in South America. These plants were long thought to have originated in Asia and Africa until archaeologists dated specimens as far back as 7,600 years old in Peru.

PINEAPPLE

Ananas comosus
BROMELIACEAE

PLANT TYPE *perennial*
GROWTH RATE *slow-growing*

METHOD *in soil*
LIGHT *low light*

WHAT IT LOOKS LIKE

The smooth, or Hawaiian, pineapple has long leaves that
are spineless. (It accounts for 75 percent of the crops
raised.) The vigorous Queen Abakka variety has narrower spiny leaves and
grows into a more exotic-looking plant than the Hawaiian type, but both
provide striking foliage plants.

If you imagine the crown of a pineapple six times bigger than it is, you
will have an idea of what a pineapple looks like growing in nature. Indoors,
a pineapple plant will grow to at least half that size. Pineapple plants die
after they flower and set fruit, but this takes several years in the home.
They are propagated by off-shoots at the base of the crown.

HOW TO GROW IT

Look for a pineapple, either Hawaiian or Abakka, with fresh center leaves
in the crown. If you have to keep a pineapple for a few days before using it,
sprinkle the crown with water to keep the leaves fresh. Twist off the crown
by holding the pineapple in one hand and the crown in the other. Then

give a mighty twist; the crown will snap right off. Carefully peel off its lower leaves until you have an inch-long stump. Note the nubs that are in horizontal bands around the stump; these are the incipient roots.

Place the crown in a large glass or jar, fill with water to cover the base of the crown, and add a teaspoon of activated charcoal. The nubs will swell in a matter of days, and the roots will form within a month.

When the pineapple's roots are 4 inches long, it is time to transplant it to a 6-inch pot. Place the pineapple in the sunniest spot in the house. Do not water until the topsoil is completely dry. The plant's roots will rot with too much water.

When the pineapple is about three years old, it is ready to bloom. The following instructions sound like witchcraft, but they work. Place the plant, pot and all, in a black plastic bag. Place half of a rotted apple flesh-side down in the crown and place the other half flesh-side down on the soil. Seal the bag for two weeks and then open to see if you can notice the beginning of growth in the center of the crown. If not, reseal the bag and wait another two weeks. Once the new growth is visible, return the pineapple to a sunny spot. It will take almost six months for the flowers to develop, but it is worth the wait! The secret? The ethylene gas that the rotting apple gives off is a growth stimulant.

ORIGIN

TROPICAL AMERICA. In 1493, Columbus saw pineapples in the West Indies, where they had been brought from South America. Within 50 years, pineapples were introduced all over the world by the Spanish and the Portuguese.

POMEGRANATE

Punica granatum

LYTHRACEAE

PLANT TYPE *deciduous shrub*	**METHOD** *from seed*
GROWTH RATE *slow-growing*	**LIGHT** *low light*

WHAT IT LOOKS LIKE

The pomegranate is a red, spherical fruit, ranging in size from 3 to 6 inches; its skin is thick and leathery. In nature, pomegranates can attain a height of 10 to 15 feet. Indoors, they can be grown on a smaller scale, and their dainty leaves and woody trunk make them an ideal subject for bonsai (decorative dwarfed trees). The fruit is available in late fall and winter in most supermarkets.

HOW TO GROW IT

Cut the fruit open and you will find lots of seeds, each inside a large, red, juicy aril (seed covering). Put on an apron and have plenty of paper towels handy. Roll the seeds gently on several thicknesses of paper towels. The red juice of the arils will squirt all over the place, but don't worry, it doesn't stain permanently. Once you've removed the arils, place the seeds on a clean towel to dry. You may plant them directly, but if you wish to store them, let the seeds dry for 24 hours and put them in an airtight jar, where they will retain their vitality for at least a year.

Sow the seeds in moist peat pellets (see Starting Plants from Seed, page 10) and place the pellets on a tray. You can also sow the seeds in a communal flat. Slip a plastic bag over the tray or flat, and give it good bottom heat. With proper heat, the seeds should germinate within 5 to 10 days. If you cannot supply bottom heat, the seeds may take more than a month to sprout.

Once they have sprouted, remove the plastic bag and place the seedlings in a warm, sunny location. Keep moist at all times. When the seedlings are 3 to 4 inches high, it is time to transplant. Pomegranates are good plants to grow under a light unit or on a southern windowsill.

Once past the seedling stage, pomegranates do not require the usual amount of humidity necessary for growing most tropical plants, which makes them ideal for the average American home that lacks humidity. When the plant is actively growing, keep the soil moist, except in the fall when it should be kept on the dry side.

To control size, pinch off the top buds. Pinching also prevents the plant from becoming spindly. When the six true leaves appear, pinch back to four leaves. Soon new branches will emerge. Pinch the branches as soon as they have six more new leaves and keep pinching until you have the shape you want. The plant will probably not fruit indoors.

SOUTHERN ASIA. Pomegranate is now naturalized throughout the Mediterranean region and in the southern United States.

If you have a garden, put your plant outside during the warmer weather. Pomegranates are hardy to Zone 7b where temperatures do not drop below 10°F. When the plant drops its leaves, bring it into a cool dark basement or unheated garage until spring.

Time to Taste

Albeit a little messy, pomegranates are delicious as a dessert fruit, and their juice is the main component of grenadine syrup. Mohammed once said, "To eat the pomegranate is to purge oneself of enemies and hate."

Sapodilla

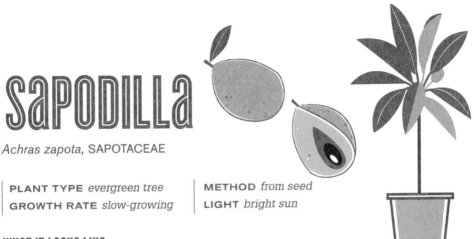

Achras zapota, SAPOTACEAE

PLANT TYPE *evergreen tree*	**METHOD** *from seed*
GROWTH RATE *slow-growing*	**LIGHT** *bright sun*

WHAT IT LOOKS LIKE

Sapodilla is sold under many different names, including chicle, naseberry, and sapote (not to be confused with black sapote, see page 97). The fruit is round to slightly oblong and about the size of a small apple. The rusty brown skin has a thin, woody texture, and when ripe, the flesh is a pale golden brown. Each fruit has five to eight shiny black seeds about ½ inch long. In its native habitat, sapodilla can attain a height of 30 to 40 feet. Indoors, a tree will grow about 6 inches a year and be compact and erect. The attractive, 3- to 4-inch-long foliage is a dark glossy green on top and pale green underneath. The fruit can be found year-round in specialty food markets.

HOW TO GROW IT

Sapodilla seeds germinate easily. They can be sown in individual peat pellets (see Starting Plants from Seed, page 10) or together in a flat. The germination process succeeds about 100 percent of the time, so plant only as many seeds as you want plants. Place a plastic bag over the tray or flat. Because sapodilla is a tropical tree, its seeds benefit from bottom heat. Germination takes 10 days to 3 weeks.

When the seeds sprout, remove the plastic bag and put the container in a bright window or under fluorescent lights. Be sure to keep the sprouts moist. When roots fill the pellets, or the seedlings in the flat have two sets of leaves, transplant to 4-inch pots. Place the pots where they will get bright light, but not direct sunlight. Keep the soil slightly moist at all times.

Early in the first year, the plant develops an attractive cinnamon-colored bark. Natural branching should occur during the second year, but if it doesn't, pinch the central bud. Grown indoors, the plant will not bear fruit.

Time To Taste

Sapodilla is a dessert fruit. Try serving it with a slice of lemon or lime. The flavor and texture are similar to that of a pear, but much sweeter.

RUBBER PIE

No fruit varies so much in quality during its different stages of ripening as does the sapodilla. When properly ripe, the sapodilla will be sweet but feel almost rotten to the touch. When firm and unripe, one bite can pucker the mouth for an hour. During the middle stages, it tastes like good old-fashioned sour apple. We once made a disastrous mistake by trying to make an "apple" pie with it at that stage. The chicle in the pulp turned it into a rubber pie. My family refers to this as "The Great Rubber Pie in the Sky."

TROPICAL AMERICA, PROBABLY SOUTHERN MEXICO. Sapodilla trees have been found growing wild throughout the West Indies and Central America. The fruit is the chief source of chicle, the base for chewing gum.

CHAPTER 4

plants from

HERBS & SPICES

Charlemagne described herbs as "the friend of physicians and the pride of the cook." And, I would humbly add, the joy of the kitchen gardener. Many are beautiful to look at and most offer a harvestable crop. When herbs and spices are used with discretion, marvelous new flavors can be added to old standard dishes.

Herbs are available everywhere and they are cheap. Most of all, they are easy to grow. The next time you are at the grocery store, look carefully inside the jars and containers of herbs and spices, and you will see that many of them contain seeds. Most will grow, some will bloom, and a few will actually yield seeds. You can easily find anise, caraway, celery, dill, fennel, sesame, and other herbs and spices while grocery shopping. (Or you can pick up seed packets at a garden center.) You do not have to send away for them.

Anise

Pimpinella anisum, APIACEAE

PLANT TYPE *annual herb*
GROWTH RATE *quick-growing*

METHOD *from seed*
LIGHT *bright sun*

WHAT IT LOOKS LIKE

The first leaves of anise are round and toothed, but later leaves are deeply lobed. The flowers, which appear later, are white, delicate, and lacy, like those of Queen Anne's lace. Outdoors, anise grows to a height of 2 feet. Indoors, it seldom reaches more than a foot tall.

HOW TO GROW IT

Start the seeds in peat pellets, sowing thickly. (See Starting Plants from Seed, page 10.) Anise seeds germinate in one week. The seedlings do not transplant well, so thin them out to one per pot when they are a few inches tall. After the seedlings have three sets of leaves, it is time to transplant them. Place each pellet in a 4-inch pot and place the pot in bright sun. To produce seeds, see Hand Pollination, page 86.

TIME TO TASTE

The seeds, which have a distinctive licorice flavor, are used in bread, pastries, candies, and liqueurs, such as anisette, Pernod, and ouzo. In India, they are used in some curries and also chewed after meals to sweeten the

breath and cure indigestion. The French favor the leaves with cooked carrots. You can also add them to salads and stews.

ORIGIN

GREECE, CRETE, AND EGYPT. The Ebers Papyrus, a famous Egyptian medical manuscript dating back to 1500 BCE, lists anise as a medicinal plant. The Greeks considered anise a medicine, and the Romans favored its use in many seasonings and sauces. The old herbals claimed that anise was both a stimulant and a relaxant, and that it was also an aromatic, diaphoretic, and tonic, besides being helpful for lung and stomach troubles. Today, anise is still used as a home remedy: anethole, the oil of anise, is used in modern cough mixtures, to help stomach ailments, and to help relieve asthma and bronchitis.

caraway

Carum carvi, APIACEAE

PLANT TYPE *annual herb*	**METHOD** *from seed*
GROWTH RATE *quick-growing*	**LIGHT** *bright sun*

WHAT IT LOOKS LIKE

Grown outdoors, caraway attains a height of 2 feet. Potbound in the home, it will be a smaller, more compact plant. The dissected, feathery foliage resembles that of the carrot plant, and its bloom resembles that of Queen Anne's lace.

HOW TO GROW IT

Caraway seedlings don't like their roots to be disturbed when transplanted, so start seeds in peat pellets, sowing generously. (See Starting Plants from Seed, page 10.) When the sprouted seedlings have three sets of leaves, you can transplant the whole peat pellets into 4-inch pots. Place the pots in a bright sunny window. When seedlings are a few inches tall, thin them out, allowing only one plant per pot. If you wish to get seeds, see Hand Pollination, page 86.

TIME TO TASTE

Caraway seed is used to flavor liqueurs and cordials, the most famous being the German kummel. The seeds are also sprinkled on rye bread and cookies and used as flavoring for pastries and cheeses. Try cooking cabbage wedges until just tender and tossing gently with butter and caraway seeds. The foliage of the young caraway plants adds a pungent and unusual flavor to soups and salads. Chop and sprinkle fresh on vegetables and meats.

ORIGIN

ASIA MINOR. Some sources claim that caraway is named after the ancient state of Caria, which is now part of Turkey, where it probably grew wild. It is one of the oldest cultivated herbs in the world; its seeds have been found around the homes of Swiss lake dwellers dating back to 5,000 BCE. For centuries, caraway was used to cure innumerable human ailments.

CELERY

easy

Apium graveolens, APIACEAE

PLANT TYPE *biennial herb*	**METHOD** *from seed*
GROWTH RATE *quick-growing*	**LIGHT** *bright sun*

WHAT IT LOOKS LIKE

Imagine the familiar, light green celery leaves growing from the stalks and you have a good idea of what the celery plant looks like. Indoors, the plant does not produce thick stalks, because these require special cultivation. Its flower is a smaller version of Queen Anne's Lace.

HOW TO GROW IT

Start celery in peat pellets (see Starting Plants from Seed, page 10), sowing generously. Keep the plants constantly moist. The seedlings will germinate in a week or two. When roots fill the pellets, plant each pellet in a 4-inch flower pot and place in a bright sunny window. Thin seedlings to one plant per pot when they are a few inches tall.

Celery is a biennial: wait two years for small white flowers. To produce your own seeds, see Hand Pollination, page 86.

ORIGIN

EUROPE AND ASIA. As a wild plant, celery grows in marshy places; as a cultivated plant, it has become transformed through the centuries from a bitter plant to the sweet, crisp vegetable we know.

CORIANDER

Coriandrum sativum

APIACEAE

PLANT TYPE *annual herb*	**METHOD** *from seed*
GROWTH RATE *quick-growing*	**LIGHT** *bright sun*

WHAT IT LOOKS LIKE

The coriander plant produces two types of leaves. The lobed, lower leaves, which look like Italian parsley leaves, contrast nicely with the finely divided, feathery, upper ones. The leaves are commonly referred to as cilantro; the seeds of the plant are the spice, coriander. Grown in a sunny window, coriander will produce clusters of lavender or pink flowers.

HOW TO GROW IT

Because the seedlings do not like to be transplanted, start the seeds in peat pellets, sowing generously. (See Starting Plants from Seed, page 10.) When roots fill the pellets, transplant each pellet to a 4-inch pot. When seedlings are a few inches high, thin them out, leaving only one per pot. If you would like to produce your own seeds indoors, see Hand Pollination, page 86.

Time to Taste

Coriander seeds are a basic ingredient in curry and chutney. Cilantro leaves are a must for many Asian, Mexican, and Indian dishes and now rival basil in popularity.

DO NOT DISTURB

Members of the Apiaceae family develop deep tap roots, which are not easily dislodged. It's therefore best to start these herbs in peat pellets, sowing the seeds generously. When plants have three sets of leaves, thin to one plant per pot. Don't try to remove young seedlings from pots, as they don't like to have their roots disturbed and therefore do not transplant easily.

ORIGIN

EUROPE AND ASIA. There is evidence of wide early use of coriander: seeds have been found in Egyptian tombs, the ancient Romans used them to preserve meat, and the Chinese were using coriander 3,000 years ago.

DILL

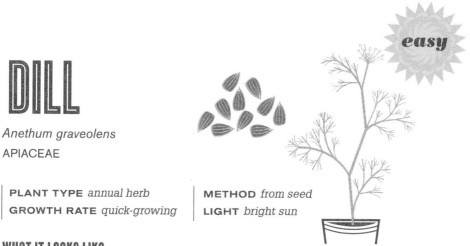

Anethum graveolens
APIACEAE

easy

PLANT TYPE *annual herb*	**METHOD** *from seed*
GROWTH RATE *quick-growing*	**LIGHT** *bright sun*

WHAT IT LOOKS LIKE

Dill has lovely, feathery foliage and clusters of greenish yellow flowers that resemble Queen Anne's lace. A healthy plant can grow 12 to 18 inches high.

HOW TO GROW IT

Because dill seedlings do not like to have their roots disturbed when transplanted, start dill seeds in peat pellets, sowing generously. (See Starting Plants from Seed, page 10.) Place the pellets on a tray and slip the tray into a plastic bag. When the seedlings sprout, usually within a week, remove the plastic bag, and put the tray in a cool, sunny window. When the roots fill the pellets, transfer them to a 4-inch flower pot. When the seedlings are a few inches tall, thin them to one plant per pot. Within two weeks you should have feathery foliage, which can be harvested, and within six weeks, clusters of flowers will develop, if the plant has had adequate sunlight. To produce your own seed, see Hand Pollination, page 86.

Time To Taste

Dill is a wonderfully versatile herb. Its foliage can be snipped into salads, soups, and dips or used in cooking fish. Use the seeds in pickles, breads, stews, and to flavor root vegetables.

ORIGIN

EUROPE AND ASIA. Used since ancient times, dill was once thought to keep people thin and to cure hiccups. Interestingly, although it has been used a remedy for insomnia, during the American Colonial period, people took dill seed to church to nibble on to keep them awake.

HAND POLLINATION

Many of the plants in this chapter are members of Apiaceae family, one that is probably best known for its Queen Anne's lace, the delicate plant with flat-topped clusters of beautiful lacy flowers that later turn to seed. Outdoor insects do the job of transferring pollen from one flower to another, but indoors you should do it yourself if you want the plant to develop seeds. If the pollen comes off on your hand when you touch the flowers, you can transfer it. Simply take a small sheet of paper and shake the flowers over it; then hold the paper above the same flowers and shake the pollen back onto them.

Fennel

Foeniculum vulgare
APIACEAE

easy

PLANT TYPE *annual herb*	**METHOD** *from seed*
GROWTH RATE *quick-growing*	**LIGHT** *bright sun*

WHAT IT LOOKS LIKE

Fennel is a graceful but rangy plant. The leaves are finely divided into threadlike, pale green segments. Fennel stalks are green-blue in color, and the flowers are a contrasting pale yellow-green.

HOW TO GROW IT

Like many other members of the Apiaceae family, fennel is difficult to transplant. Therefore, start seeds in peat pellets (see Starting Plants from Seed, page 10), sowing generously. When the seedlings are a few inches tall, thin them out, leaving only one plant per pellet. When roots fill the pellets, transplant them to 4-inch pots.

Fennel needs full sun and lots of water, but it is relatively hardy and can be grown on a cool windowsill. The flowers appear in about six weeks. If you wish to harvest seeds, see Hand Pollination on page 86. One *umbel*, or cluster of flowers, alone can yield 20 to 30 seeds.

Time to Taste

Fennel leaves have a delicate licorice flavor; use them in salads, sauces, soups, and meat dishes. The seeds contain a volatile oil that is used to flavor bread, pastry, candy, liqueurs, and meat. Indian restaurants frequently offer bowls of candied fennel seeds to refresh the breath and mouth after a meal.

ORIGIN

EUROPEAN SHORES OF THE MEDITERRANEAN. Fennel has been cultivated for more than 3,000 years. The Greek word for fennel is *maratho*. Allegedly Greek marathon runners had to run through fields of maratho, hence the word *marathon*. In Ancient Greece and Rome, victorious warriors and athletes received crowns of fennel sprigs.

FENUGREEK

Trigonella foenum-graecum
FABACEAE

PLANT TYPE *annual herb*
GROWTH RATE *quick-growing*

METHOD *from seed*
LIGHT *bright sun*

WHAT IT LOOKS LIKE

Fenugreek is a small, attractive, trailing plant with leaves that resemble those of the pea family and small, white pealike flowers. The flowers are followed shortly by small pods that look like elf shoes. The seeds are available year-round in spice stores and health food stores.

HOW TO GROW IT

Fill a 6-inch pot three-quarters full with moist potting soil. Place several seeds on the surface and cover with ¼ inch of soil. Slip a plastic bag over the pot and set it in a warm place. When the seeds germinate (in 3 to 10 days) remove the plastic and place in a sunny window. Because fenugreek trails, try placing the pot in a hanging basket.

Flowers appear within eight weeks. The plant self-pollinates and the pods appear shortly afterward.

Time to Taste

Fenugreek seeds are an exotic spice found in almost all Middle and Far Eastern markets. They are a component of curry in India, and in Turkey and Iraq are combined with paprika to preserve meat. Use seeds in chicken stock, scatter them in the bottom of roasting pans with pork or chicken to enrich the gravy, and best of all, insert the seeds in lamb before roasting.

ORIGIN

SOUTHERN EUROPE AND ASIA. In Greek, the word literally means "Greek hay." Although the plant bears no resemblance to hay, it is used for fodder in much of the Mediterranean region. In Tunisia, flour made from fenugreek seeds was used for putting on weight, and young brides were fattened up, prior to their weddings.

MUSTARD

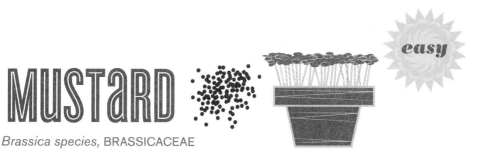

Brassica species, BRASSICACEAE

PLANT TYPE *annual herb*
GROWTH RATE *quick-growing*

METHOD *from seed*
LIGHT *bright sun*

WHAT IT LOOKS LIKE

Mustard foliage is rough and crumpled looking, but attractive. The plant will produce four-petaled yellow flowers and, when not crowded, grow to a height of 2 feet.

HOW TO GROW IT

Fill a shallow container three-quarters full with moist potting soil. Scatter a tablespoonful of seeds evenly on the soil's surface and cover with a light dusting of soil. Slip a plastic bag over the container and put it in a warm, sunny window. The seeds germinate rapidly. Remove the bag when the seedlings are 4 inches high.

You can keep the container of seedlings as an attractive plant or, if you want to grow a plant to maturity, remove one seedling from the container

ORIGIN

EUROPE AND ASIA. Since antiquity, mustard seeds have been used to cure ailments as well as to preserve perishables. Mustard poultices are still used as a household remedy for bronchitis and muscular aches.

and transplant it to a 4-inch pot filled with potting soil. Take care to gently loosen the soil underneath the seedling with a pencil and lift the plant out by the leaves. (A plant can always regenerate new leaves but not a stem.) Use a pencil to make a hole deep enough to receive the roots, and cover about an inch of the stem with soil. Water well and place the pot in a sunny window. If your light is good, the plant will produce flowers.

Time to Taste

Mustard has many uses. Cut the leaves when the plant is 3 inches high and use as a garnish for steaks, salads, and soups. The larger, older leaves can be cooked like spinach, but you will find that mustard greens have a much tangier taste. Grind the seed to make mustard powder, and use the whole seed as a pickling spice.

sesame

Sesamum indicum
PEDALIACEAE

easy

PLANT TYPE *annual herb*	**METHOD** *from seed*
GROWTH RATE *quick-growing*	**LIGHT** *bright sun*

WHAT IT LOOKS LIKE

Although attractive, the sesame plant may seem somewhat weedy-looking. Its leaves are oval and slightly hairy. The tubular flowers are pinkish-white and resemble foxglove. These are followed by seed capsules.

HOW TO GROW IT

Purchase unhulled from health food stores and spice shops, not the polished seed found in supermarkets. Fill a shallow container three-quarters full with moist potting soil. Scatter a tablespoonful of seeds evenly on the surface and cover the seeds with a light dusting of soil. Slip a plastic bag over the container and place in a sunny window.

The seeds germinate rapidly and will be several inches high in two weeks. Sesame plants are most attractive when crowded together in their original container. They can stay this way for months.

If you want to grow a plant to maturity, you must transplant one seedling at to a 6-inch pot. Flowers are self-pollinating and will be followed by seed capsules that pop open when ripe.

Time to Taste

Sesame seeds have a nutty taste and are scattered over bread and cakes or used in candies and desserts. Ground seeds are a component of halvah, a famous sweet of the Middle East, and tahini, which is used in salad dressings or to flavor hummus. The oil expressed from the seeds is an excellent salad oil and is much used in Japan.

ORIGIN

ASIA AND AFRICA. The famous phrase "open sesame" probably comes from the fact that the seed capsules split open when ripe. Because the leaves are mucilaginous and sticky, they were used as a remedy for dysentery and diarrhea.

CHAPTER 5
plants from LATIN AMERICA

When Milly and I set forth from our Manhattan apartments on our first field trip in pursuit of Latin American tubers, we struck gold within two blocks in a small Puerto Rican grocery store. There we found glorious boxes full of many different tubers. Milly, the botanist, peeled back the skin of each type in search of the growing end and to evaluate the viability of each tuber. The proprietors found her behavior somewhat alarming and soon we had a curious audience.

Milly's Spanish vocabulary was limited to "What is it?" and "How do you spell it?" Neither went very far to explain her actions, but she did manage to convince them that we were harmless, albeit a little crazy. Soon we were all chatting in a combination of English and Spanish. Milly and I each purchased two of each tuber, one to eat and one to grow.

One fact, at least, emerged during our field trip — some tubers have several different names. The vegetable I called *malanga*, Milly called *dasheen* and the proprietor called *yautia*. The owners assured us that all the names are correct; some were Puerto Rican, others Mexican, and some Spanish. Our taxonomy in this chapter is based on L. H. Bailey's *Cyclopedia of Horticulture*. Whenever possible the names used by a variety of cultures are provided.

BLACK SAPOTE

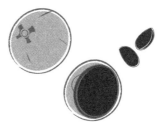

Diospyros digyna
EBENACEAE

PLANT TYPE *evergreen tree*
GROWTH RATE *slow-growing*

METHOD *from seed*
LIGHT *bright sun*

WHAT IT LOOKS LIKE

The name black sapote is confusing because this fruit is neither black on the outside nor is it related to sapodilla, one of whose alternative names is *sapote*. When you buy black sapote in the store, it looks like a small green

persimmon. The flesh is black when ripe and looks like axle grease. Within the dark pulpy mass are six, large, flat, brown seeds about a ½ inch long and wide.

The most outstanding feature of the young black sapote plant is its hard, black trunk. Black sapote is in the same family as ebony. The new leaves are a dark glossy green, oblong, and slightly pointed, and they contrast handsomely with the dark bark.

The fruit is available in some Latin markets and off and on throughout the year in some parts of the South.

HOW TO GROW IT

Remove the seeds from the fruit's flesh and rinse them. Start the seeds in a flat filled with moistened potting soil, large enough to contain them. Gently tamp down the soil in the flat and then make holes in the soil deep enough to plant the seeds. Slip a plastic bag over the flat and give it bottom heat. The seeds germinate rapidly (in 10 days to 3 weeks) and germination is close to 100 percent.

When the seedlings emerge from the soil, the stems look like brown loops, but soon the stems straighten out and leaves appear. At this point, remove the plastic bag and put the seedlings in a sunny window.

When the seedlings have their second set of leaves, it is time to transplant them into 4-inch pots, each filled three-quarters full with moist potting soil. Loosen the soil around the seedlings and carefully lift each out, holding onto a leaf. Make a hole in the soil, deep enough to contain the roots, and place the seedling in. Put the pots in a sunny window and keep the soil moist at all times.

Black sapotes grow relatively slowly, less than a foot a year. Older plants should be transplanted to 6-inch pots, when the roots show through the bottom. With patience it is possible for your plant to flower and bear fruit.

TIME TO TASTE

The black sapote is frequently referred to as the "chocolate pudding tree" because of the color of its flesh and the hint of chocolate in its flavor. When the fruit is fully ripe (it will feel almost rotten to the touch), try mixing it with a little sour cream and creme de cacao and serving it as a sauce or pudding. You can also follow recipes for persimmon puddings and cakes and replace the persimmon with black sapote.

ORIGIN

MEXICO AND CENTRAL AMERICA. Black sapote is believed to have been cultivated by the indigenous people of the Americas since 4,000 BCE. Today it is commercially grown for its wood.

CHAYOTE

Sechium edule
CUCURBITACEAE

PLANT TYPE *perennial vine*	**METHOD** *in soil*
GROWTH RATE *quick-growing*	**LIGHT** *bright sun*

WHAT IT LOOKS LIKE

The fruit is green or cream-colored and resembles a deeply ribbed squash. The seed usually protrudes at the upper end of the fruit. Frequently, the seeds are already sprouting when you buy the fruit. The chayote is a vigorous vine. In nature, it is grown on large arbors much like grapes and can grow 50 feet in one season. Indoors, chayote can easily cover a window with its cucumber-like lobed leaves. Outdoors, the vine will produce flowers and edible underground tubers that are prized in South America. The fruit is available year-round in Latin American grocery stores.

HOW TO GROW IT

Plant the entire fruit horizontally, with the stem end just under the soil surface, in a soil-filled pot big enough to contain it. Slip a plastic bag over the pot to retain humidity and put it in a warm place. When you see growth starting, remove the plastic bag and put the pot in a bright or sunny window. Keep the plant well-watered and fertilize it often with liquid fertilizer. Leaves will soon appear.

Time to Taste

Chayote can be cooked like summer squash.

MEXICO AND GUATEMALA. Chayote was cultivated by the indigenous peoples of Central America long before the discovery of America by Europeans.

CHERIMOYA

Annona cherimola, ANNONACEAE

PLANT TYPE *deciduous tree*	**METHOD** *from seed*
GROWTH RATE *slow-growing*	**LIGHT** *bright sun*

WHAT IT LOOKS LIKE

The heart-shaped, gray-green fruit of the cherimoya can range in size from 8 ounces to 6 pounds. About 25 black seeds, ¾ inch long and pointed at one end, are buried in the creamy white flesh of the fruit. The tree has a graceful quality that makes it a treasured indoor plant. The fruit is available during the winter in specialty food stores and supermarkets.

HOW TO GROW IT

Remove the seeds from the fruit's flesh. Start in moistened peat pellets or a sphagnum bag. (See Starting Plants from Seed, page 10, and The Secret of the Sphagnum Bag, page 8.) Because you can expect 95 percent germination, plant the same number of seeds as you want of plants. (Dry unused seeds overnight and place them in an airtight container. They will retain their vitality for several years.) If using peat pellets, slip a plastic bag over the pellet tray. Place the tray where it can receive bottom heat. Seeds will sprout in one to three weeks.

When seedlings appear, remove the plastic bag and put the container in a bright window or under lights. If using a sphagnum bag, harden off the plants and transplant into containers. When a seedling emerges, it is looped over like a swan with its head in the water. Soon the seed pod appears on a 3-inch-long neck and just sits there for several weeks while the leaves slowly develop, one by one. It is not unusual to see a seedling with six fully developed, pale-green leaves and remnants of the seed pod still on the plant. It is a temptation to remove the silly-looking thing, but leave it alone.

When the seedlings have two sets of leaves, transplant each to a 4-inch flower pot filled with moist potting soil. Place the pots in a bright window or under lights. When the plants grow too big for their pots (roots come through the hole in the bottom), move them to 6-inch pots.

The cherimoya tree grows about 8 inches a year but does not bear fruit indoors. It has a gently curving stem that needs to be pinched back in order to develop a branched and compact shape. Some kinds of cherimoya are deciduous (that is, they drop their leaves). Should your plant shed its leaves in the late fall, just water it less. It will leaf out again after this dormant period.

Time to Taste

Cherimoya is the queen of the tropical fruits of the New World. Its texture is like that of custard, and its flavor is a combination of strawberry, pineapple, banana, and yogurt. It makes a delicious dessert fruit, as well as a soothing, refreshing drink when pureed. (If you lace the drink with brandy, you have dessert and cordial all in one.) One hot day in Miami, we were served a high tea of cherimoya shake along with a slice of chilled mango on pound cake. We doubt any tea was ever so refreshing.

ORIGIN

TROPICAL AMERICA. The cherimoya may well be the oldest cultivated fruit in the New World; pottery urns in the shape of cherimoyas have been unearthed from ancient burial grounds in Peru. Today, cherimoya are grown throughout the tropical world, as well as in the state of California.

GENIP

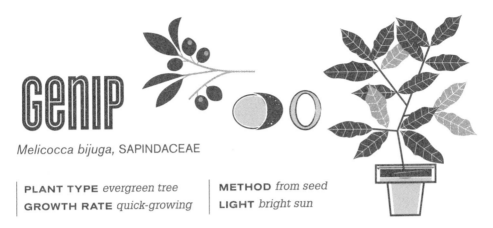

Melicocca bijuga, SAPINDACEAE

PLANT TYPE *evergreen tree*	**METHOD** *from seed*
GROWTH RATE *quick-growing*	**LIGHT** *bright sun*

WHAT IT LOOKS LIKE

Genips are sold under several different names, including Spanish lime, knepe, and queenpea. The fruit bears no resemblance to a lime in texture, taste, or appearance, and it is not a member of the citrus family.

Genips are sold in twiggy, rather unattractive clusters. The individual fruit is round and about 1 inch in diameter, with gray-green skin that makes it look like a leathery grape. It splits open easily, revealing cream-colored, translucent flesh surrounding one large seed the size of a peanut.

The plant is most noteworthy for its very unusual light green foliage. It has several large, ruffled leaflets that rise from a 6- to 8-inch leaf stalk. The plant's shape is compact.

It is available in spring in Chinese, Japanese, and Spanish markets.

HOW TO GROW IT

Carefully chew the sweet flesh from the seed. These seeds can easily be grown in a flat or in a sphagnum bag (See The Secret of the Sphagnum Bag, page 8). If using a flat, slip a plastic bag over it and provide good bottom heat.

Seeds germinate rapidly, in 10 days to 2 weeks. When the first leaves appear, remove the plastic bag from the flat, or if begun in sphagnum, plant in a small pot, and place the seedlings in a warm bright spot. Provide as much humidity as possible and never allow the seedlings to dry out. When seedlings are 3 or 4 inches high or have two sets of leaves, it is time to transplant them.

Genip grows roughly 10 to 12 inches a year. The plant's shape is so compact that pinching and pruning are not really necessary to achieve a well-shaped plant.

Time To Taste

The fruits are eaten fresh. The slightly fibrous flesh has a flavor that is a cross between that of a grape and a mango. It is very refreshing on a hot day. The seeds, when roasted like chestnuts, taste very much like peanuts.

ORIGIN

NORTHERN SOUTH AMERICA, CENTRAL AMERICA, AND THE WEST INDIES. In Cuba, cowboys carried bunches of genips on their saddle horns to quench their thirst. Today, genips are grown commercially in southern Florida and southern California.

easy

Jicama

Pachyrhizus erosus
FABACEAE

PLANT TYPE *perennial vine*	**METHOD** *in soil*
GROWTH RATE *quick-growing*	**LIGHT** *bright sun*

WHAT IT LOOKS LIKE

Jicama, a member of the morning glory family, is a vine whose root looks like a large, dusty, brown top. The roots vary greatly in size, from 4 to 8 inches across. It makes a lovely, trailing plant.

HOW TO GROW IT

Place the pointed end of a root in a glass or jar of water just large enough to support it, with the bottom 2 inches of the root immersed in water. Place in a warm spot in your house.

Within one to two weeks, white bumps (the roots) appear all over the bottom. It may take a month or more to develop a healthy root system, after which time stems develop and the jicama shrinks perceptibly in size. Once the glass or jar is filled with roots, it is time to transplant. Fill an 8-inch pot one-third full with a moist potting soil. Place the root on the soil and fill in around it,

ORIGIN

TROPICAL AMERICA.
The word jicama derives from the Aztec word *xicamatl.*

allowing the top inch of the root to show above the surface. Place the pot in a bright sunny window.

In about six to eight weeks, fuzzy, leafless stems develop. The plant then needs a couple of more weeks to become a full, leafy plant.

Time to Taste

Jicama has a crunchy texture and a sweet taste similar to that of a water chestnut. Try it by itself with a squirt of lime juice and a few pinches of sugar and chile powder, or add it to a crudité tray or salad. All plant parts except the roots contain rotenone, which is processed and used as a pesticide.

MALANGA

Xanthosoma sagittifolium, ARACEAE

PLANT TYPE *perennial tuber*	**METHOD** *in soil*
GROWTH RATE *quick-growing*	**LIGHT** *bright sun*

WHAT IT LOOKS LIKE

The Latin American malanga is a pinkish brown tuber ranging in size from 4 to 10 inches in length and 2 to 3 inches in width. Banded by narrow, horizontal, gray stripes, it usually tapers to a tip at one end. The name *malanga* is used interchangeably with the names *yautia* and *dasheen*, but don't confuse this fruit with the dasheen sold in Chinese markets (see Taro, page 147).

In nature, malangas grow in jungles or open fields. Indoors, the malanga develops into a compact, leafy plant, seldom exceeding 12 inches in height. The leaves are a soft green and range from 2 to 6 inches long. Each leaf develops from the main stalk; as one leaf matures, another peels off from the same stalk.

The fruit is available year-round in Latin American and Asian markets.

HOW TO GROW IT

Start the tuber in a sphagnum bag. (See The Secret of the Sphagnum Bag, page 8.) Check the bag every three or four days for any soft spots that might develop on the tuber and cut them out at once.

In one to three weeks pointed pink buds sprout all over the malanga tuber. When the buds are 1 to 2 inches long, it is time to plant the tuber. Use a shallow pot that is wide enough to accommodate it, with an inch to spare all around. Fill half of the pot with moist potting soil. Place the tuber horizontally on the surface, fill in around it, and barely cover it with more moist soil. Don't worry about the sprouts you have buried; they will work their way to the surface. During its early stages of growth, malanga needs high humidity and warmth. Once you have planted the tuber, cover the pot with a plastic bag and put it in a warm spot. When a few of the buds turn into leaves, you may remove the plastic bag and place the pot in a bright window. It grows quickly.

If you have a garden, malanga does well in summer in a shady spot or in a tub on the terrace, as long as there is plenty of warmth and moisture. It may produce new small tubers underground.

Time to Taste

Prepare malanga as you would a sweet potato: boil, peel, and mash. The vegetable has a pleasant nutty flavor. Add lots of butter, salt, pepper, and a dash of orange juice to mask a sometimes slight sulfuric taste. *Caution: Do not eat the poisonous leaves of the plant.*

ORIGIN

SOUTH AND CENTRAL AMERICA. There are more than 40 species of malanga, some of which are among the oldest root crops in the world. It is especially popular in Cuba and Puerto Rico.

PRICKLY PEAR

Opuntia ficus-indica
CACTACEAE

| **PLANT TYPE** *perennial* | **METHOD** *in soil* |
| **GROWTH RATE** *slow-growing* | **LIGHT** *bright light* |

WHAT IT LOOKS LIKE

Brick-red in color, the fruit is about the size of a large hen's egg. When picked fresh, it is covered with minute spines, but most of these have been removed from those sold commercially. The flesh is a deep pink, with many small black seeds. In nature, the prickly pear can grow to be 15 feet tall. Grown indoors, it will be much smaller and not bear fruit. The leaves look like fleshy pads. The fruit is available during the spring and summer in gourmet shops and some supermarkets.

HOW TO GROW IT

Scoop out a dozen or more seeds from the fruit and wash off any flesh clinging to them. Plant them immediately in a flat, using barely moist potting soil. The seeds are small and need only to be dusted with a thin layer of soil. Cover the flat with plastic and provide good bottom heat.

Germination of prickly pear is erratic; the time period can range from 10 days to more than 2 months for seeds from one batch. Do not discard the flat after a few seeds have germinated; many more will be on the way.

Once the first seedlings have sprouted, move the flat to a warm, sunny place or to a light unit. Keep the flat covered until a good proportion of the seeds have germinated. Seedlings require careful watering. Do not allow the seed bed to dry out.

When the seedlings are an inch high and a distinctive spiny leaf has developed on each, they may be transplanted into 1-inch pots. Gently loosen the soil under each seedling with a pencil and lift it out by the leaves. For each seedling, fill a pot with moist potting soil and use the pencil to make a hole deep enough to receive the roots. Cover about a ¼ inch of the stem with soil. When roots fill the pots, transplant to 4-inch pots.

Young plants bear no resemblance to mature ones, and you may well wonder what has sprouted in your seed bed. At first, two fleshy, spineless leaves appear. Within two weeks, you will notice tiny green bristles developing between the leaves. These are the beginning of the first true leaves, which are fleshy pads. The prickly pear grows slowly, developing at the rate of one pad every six months. It is most attractive when small.

It is also possible to grow prickly pear from one of its pads. Cut the leaf in half horizontally and allow it to dry overnight. Fill a container with barely moist soil and bury one-third of the leaf. It will begin to root in a week or two. Transplant to a 4-inch pot when the roots are about 4 inches long (when you see the roots beginning to appear at the hole in the bottom of the pot).

Time to Taste

Prickly pears combine the delicious flavors of the watermelon and the strawberry. To serve, simply cut them horizontally and scoop out the flesh. The pads of the prickly pear are also edible. The pads, known in Mexico as *nopales,* must first be thoroughly cleaned of all spines. Then either boil, grill, or fry, and add to salads and other Mexican dishes.

ORIGIN

CENTRAL AND SOUTH AMERICA. It is generally believed that Columbus introduced the prickly pear fruit to the Old World. Today it is extensively cultivated in North Africa and Sicily; in the United States it is grown in the Southwest.

TAMARILLO

Cyphomandra betacea, SOLANACEAE

PLANT TYPE *tree*
GROWTH RATE *slow-growing*

METHOD *from seed*
LIGHT *bright sun*

WHAT IT LOOKS LIKE

Tamarillo, or tree tomato, is a semi-woody, small tree that seldom exceeds 10 feet in height. It has large, blue-green, heart-shaped leaves that are 4 to 6 inches in length. Its ½-inch flowers are white tinged with purple and resemble tomato flowers. These are followed by 4-inch, egg-shaped fruits that are either scarlet or orange. The fruits have long stems that dangle down below the large leaves; inside these are dozens of small, flat, white seeds. The fruit is available May through September in specialty food markets.

HOW TO GROW IT

Some seeds, because of their small size or the stickiness of their flesh, are difficult to clean on a paper towel. Tamarillo seeds are a good example. These seeds are best cleaned by fermentation. Scoop out the seeds and remove as much of the flesh as you can. Put the seeds into a small container of water and soak for a couple of days. Most of the remaining flesh will rise to the top. Drain the seeds and rub on a paper towel. The seeds, when dry, can be stored in an airtight container for months, or they can be sown immediately in a large flat or in individual peat pellets. (See Starting Plants from Seed, page 10.) Cover the flat or group of pellets with a plastic bag. Place in a bright, sunny window and keep evenly moist at all times.

When seedlings are 4 inches tall, transplant them to individual 4-inch pots. A seedling tamarillo is somewhat floppy and not too promising. Have patience: Your ugly duckling will soon look like a large, tropical anthurium. With proper care, your plant will bear fruit in two to three years.

Time to Taste

Some recipes state tamarillos can be used as a substitute for tomatoes. You should usually peel the fruit as you would a tomato before use. Try sprinkling sugar over them, putting in the fridge overnight, and serving chilled with a sherry sauce. Scoop the flesh from the skin.

 ORIGIN

PERU, CHILE, ECUADOR, AND BOLIVIA. From these places tamarillo spread to other South American countries, as well as to New Zealand, where it is widely cultivated.

TOMATILLO

Physalis ixocarpa, SOLANACEAE

PLANT TYPE *annual*	**METHOD** *from seed*
GROWTH RATE *quick-growing*	**LIGHT** *bright sun*

WHAT IT LOOKS LIKE

The tomatillo has an identity crisis: It looks like one plant and sounds like another. It looks identical to Chinese lantern (*Physalis alkekengi*), a handsome but poisonous weed, when the plants are immature. (Once, a friend of mine who was helping me weed, pulled up all of my tomatillo plants, thinking they were Chinese lanterns.) Mature Chinese lanterns have a bright orange husk surrounding a ½-inch fruit, but the tomatillo has a brownish papery husk that clings to its firm, round fruit.

The name sounds like tamarillo (*Cyphomandra betacea*), or tree tomato (see page 114). Tamarillos, however, are bright orange or red and about the size and shape of an egg; they are the fruit of a tree.

The fruit is available year-round in Latin American markets and some supermarkets.

HOW TO GROW IT

The tomatillo is green when it is sold and used in cooking. The seeds are immature at this stage. To ripen the fruit, put it in a brown paper bag with an apple. The fruit is mature when it has turned yellow. At this point, remove and use the seeds. The seeds are tiny and should be fermented (see Cleaning Seeds, page 10).

Seeds germinate in about a week. When the seedlings have two sets of leaves, transplant them to individual pots. If the weather is warm at the time, grow them in the garden where they will re-sow for the next year. The plants will grow to be 3 or 4 feet high.

TIME TO TASTE

Tomatillos have a tangy taste, albeit a little sour. They are the basis of salsa verde, which is used in Mexican cooking.

ORIGIN

CENTRAL AMERICA. It was first domesticated by the Aztecs and dates back to at least 800 BCE.

TROPICAL GUAVA

Psidium guajava, MYRTACEAE

PLANT TYPE *evergreen tree/shrub*	**METHOD** *from seed*
GROWTH RATE *slow-growing*	**LIGHT** *bright sun*

easy

Tropical guava makes a handsome houseplant, but best of all, it flowers and fruits. It is available during the fall in specialty food stores.

WHAT IT LOOKS LIKE

Tropical guava is a small, evergreen tree. Its fruit is egg-shaped, yellow-green, and ripe when the flesh yields to the touch, much as a peach does. The fruit varies in size from 2 to 4 inches. In nature, the tree grows to 25 feet. It is much smaller when grown in a container. The leaves are a dark glossy green and the 1-inch white flowers are fragrant. The plant thrives in a sunny, humid atmosphere.

HOW TO GROW IT

Remove seeds from the fruit and clean by fermenting (see Cleaning Seeds, page 10). The seeds can be sown immediately or dried and stored in an airtight jar for several months. Sow the seeds in a large flat, cover the flat with plastic, and put in a warm, bright location in the house. The seeds germinate in a couple of weeks.

When seedlings have two sets of leaves, transplant them to individual 4-inch pots. It takes about three years to bring the guava into bloom. Be sure to transplant when needed, and you must bring them outdoors in the summer if you want flowers and fruit.

TIME TO TASTE

Guavas are delicious when eaten fresh. They are high in pectin and also make excellent preserves.

ORIGIN

PERU AND BRAZIL. Early Portuguese and Spanish explorers carried guava to the East Indies and Guam, where it spread through the warm parts of Asia and Africa.

STRAWBERRY GUAVA

Psidium littorale
MYRTACEAE

There are two types of guava: the tropical and the strawberrry guava. The strawberry guava is a handsome evergreen shrub with deeply veined, dark green leaves that set off small, fragrant, white flowers. In warmer parts of the United States, such as Hawaii and Florida, strawberry guava is grown as a landscape specimen or used to form hedges. It is much hardier than the tropical guava and can withstand a few days of frost. (*Beware:* It is very invasive.)

To grow strawberry guava, follow the instructions for tropical guava. Like the tropical variety, the strawberry guava fruits and is available during the fall in specialty food stores.

CHAPTER 6 · plants from ASIA

Asian markets are among the most glorious sources of unusual fresh fruits and vegetables to grow: taro, ginger, water chestnuts, bitter melon, litchi, jujube, and many other fruits and nuts.

Some excellent Asian produce can be purchased in supermarkets, but generally, large grocery stores cater to the novice American appetite. For really unusual goodies, go to the small shops. The merchandise is just as fresh and much more varied.

Middle Eastern markets have an aura all their own. The air is perfumed with the aroma of cinnamon, clove, fenugreek, and other exotic odors. There are bins of nearly every kind of dried bean imaginable and all but the split peas will grow. And there are many wonderful dried fruits. One of my favorite purchases is tamarind paste (see Tamarind, page 145).

ARROWHEAD

Sagittaria chinensis
ALISMATACEAE

PLANT TYPE *perennial corm*	**METHOD** *in pebbles/in water*
GROWTH RATE *quick-growing*	**LIGHT** *low light*

WHAT IT LOOKS LIKE

Arrowhead is a tall, erect plant with 6- to 8-inch-wide, arrow-shaped leaves. Its stalks can reach a height of 4 feet, even in the home. The flowers are white and fragrant and highly prized. The arrowhead is an aquatic perennial and is often used in aquatic gardens as an ornamental plant. It is available three to four weeks in late fall in Asian markets.

HOW TO GROW IT

The plant grows from a corm that looks somewhat like a tulip bulb. These corms are in the market for such a short time that you really have to keep an eye out for them. Choose firm ones with a spike, showing some growth at the top. In nature, the plant grows in the rich alluvial soil of sluggish rivers and ponds. To duplicate this soil, use a rich mixture of three parts potting soil and one part sand or bird gravel. Add a tablespoonful of fish

ORIGIN

THE TEMPERATE AND SUBTROPICAL REGIONS OF ASIA

fertilizer, then add water until you have the consistency of mud. The mixture will have a slight odor similar to the smell of the ocean at low tide.

Put 1 inch of the mud mixture into the bottom of a small empty aquarium. Place the corms on top and cover with 2 inches of sand or gravel. Add enough water so that is 1 inch above the soil level. Arrowheads grown this way send out stems lying on or just below the soil surface and rapidly form new corms. If a plant becomes too big, you can easily cut the connected corms apart and remove some.

Try growing arrowhead corms on pebbles as well. (See Starting Plants in Pebbles, page 9.)

Time to Taste

Arrowhead corms are a starchy vegetable with a flavor similar to sweet potatoes. Cook similarly: boil, peel, and mash.

BITTER MELON

Momordica charantia, CUCURBITACEAE

PLANT TYPE *annual vine*
GROWTH RATE *quick-growing*

METHOD *from seed*
LIGHT *bright sun*

easy

WHAT IT LOOKS LIKE

You cannot mistake this unusually shaped fruit. A soft, gray-green color, it is 6 to 8 inches long, tapered at both ends, and covered with smooth warts in longitudinal bands. As it ripens, bitter melon turns into a brilliant orange and makes a handsome addition to a fruit-bowl centerpiece.

The plant is a graceful vine with deeply lobed leaves and small yellow blooms. It supports itself by means of tendrils that wrap themselves around any support you provide.

The fruit is available year-round in Asian markets.

HOW TO GROW IT

Remove the red aril (seed covering) from the seed; it should peel off easily. Fill a 6-inch hanging basket with moist potting soil to within an inch of the rim and plant three seeds inside. Cover the seeds with a ½ inch of soil, then put a sheet of plastic over the top of the pot and move it to a warm place. Seeds will germinate within a week. At that point, remove the plastic and hang the pot in a bright or sunny window. Water frequently; the bitter melon grows quickly. Try training the vines to wind upward along the supporting wires of the hanging basket and let succeeding branches trail down.

Bitter melons are also marvelous plants to frame a window. To do this, plant in a pot and provide string supports along the sides of your window. In a brightly lit window, you will soon have a beautiful natural drapery of leaves. It flowers with small yellow blooms.

You can get bitter melon to fruit and seed by following the pollinating directions on page 86. Do not be discouraged by this annual's limited life; these beautiful plants grow quickly and easily.

TIME TO TASTE

"Bitter" melon is an understatement. The fruit has a distinctive, intensely bitter flavor. It is often used in soups and with beef and to accent bland dishes. The red aril surrounding the seed is sweet and considered a great delicacy in Chinese cooking. *Caution:* Avoid the poisonous seeds.

ORIGIN

AFRICA AND TROPICAL ASIA. Bitter melon is grown in the southern parts of the United States as an ornamental vine.

DAiKON

Raphanus longipinatus
BRASSICACEAE

PLANT TYPE *annual root*	**METHOD** *in water*
GROWTH RATE *quick-growing*	**LIGHT** *low light*

WHAT IT LOOKS LIKE

The daikon, also known as Japanese white radish, is a long, dull white root 8 to 12 inches in length and 2 to 3 inches in width. It can reach an astounding 20 pounds. The daikon produces lovely, lush, curled foliage, with leaves that are 10 to 18 inches long.

HOW TO GROW IT

Jars large enough to accommodate this root are hard to find, so cut a root to the size that will fit whatever you have available. Stick bamboo skewers into the skin of the root about one-third of the way down from the top. Fill the jar with water and add a tablespoon of activated charcoal (see Starting Plants in Water, page 7) to the water. Place the root in the jar, allowing the skewers to rest on the rim. Keep adding water to replenish the water that evaporates.

ORIGIN

CHINA AND JAPAN. In Japanese, its name means "large root"; in Chinese, its name means "white radish."

Foliage appears within two weeks. It is hard for daikons to bloom indoors, but the plant's long, curled foliage more than makes up for this deficiency.

Time to Taste

This plant is milder than the common garden radish and is used in Asian cooking chiefly to dip into sauces or as an ingredient in mixed vegetable dishes.

easy

GINGER

Zingiber officinale
ZINGIBERACEAE

PLANT TYPE *perennial rhizome*	**METHOD** *in soil*
GROWTH RATE *quick-growing*	**LIGHT** *indirect sunlight*

WHAT IT LOOKS LIKE

Ginger is an underground stem, called a rhizome, that has buds that grow into stems and narrow leaves. The pure white flowers are delightfully fragrant. They are borne in a leafy conelike structure at the end of a cane that holds as many as 15 blooms.

HOW TO GROW IT

Select a shallow, wide pot large enough to accommodate the rhizome. Fill three quarters of the pot with moist potting soil and lay the rhizome on top of the soil. Keep the soil moist and put the pot in a place that is brightly lit but not sunny. Use bottom heat to hasten germination.

The ginger plant grows tall quickly and resembles a stand of bamboo. In six weeks it can be as tall as 3 feet. As the old stalks die, new ones sprout. A healthy ginger plant should continue to sprout for

ORIGIN

TROPICAL ASIA. Ginger is now cultivated throughout the tropical world.

several months. If you have a garden, put the plant outside for the summer. This can encourage blooms. Individual flowers last only a day or two but are followed by more.

Time to Taste

Gingerroot has a sweetish, tangy flavor and is used often in Asian cooking. To use ginger, carefully slice off about an inch from the end of the rhizome and peel off the skin.

JUJUBE

Ziziphus jujuba
RHAMNACEAE

PLANT TYPE *deciduous tree*
GROWTH RATE *quick-growing*

METHOD *from seed*
LIGHT *bright sun*

WHAT IT LOOKS LIKE

The jujube, or Chinese red date, has no relationship to the familiar African date palm. The small, reddish brown fruit is the size of a kumquat. It is usually sold dried in plastic bags, and you can get a hundred for a few dollars. The jujube plant has small, shiny, silver-green leaves. The fruit is available year-round in Asian markets.

HOW TO GROW IT

Carefully chew off all the flesh from the hard central seed of a few jujubes. The seeds then need to be stratified in containers. (See When "Cold" Is a Good Thing, page 12.) Germination takes 10 days to 3 weeks from the time you remove the seeds from the refrigerator. The seeds can remain in their containers until they germinate. Once the seeds have developed roots and a stem, transplant them to 4-inch pots. Place the pots in a warm, sunny window or under a light unit. Seedlings must be kept moist.

For an attractive, bushy plant, pinch the stems when the plant is 4 inches tall and continue pinching succeeding branches; otherwise, you end up with a rather spindly plant. The jujube, with its small leaves and early blooms, could be grown as a bonsai (a dwarfed tree shaped by pinching and pruning).

Move jujube to a spot in the garden, patio, or balcony, if you have one, after all danger of frost has past. Keep in the garden until the plant drops its leaves in the fall and then move it to a cool basement or garage for its dormant period. The jujube is hardy to USDA zone 7a (5°F).

Time to Taste
Jujubes are eaten fresh or semidried.

CHINA AND POSSIBLY SYRIA.
ORIGIN
Jujube has been cultivated in China for more than 4,000 years and there are more than 400 Chinese cultivars.

Lemongrass

Cymbopogon citratus, POACEAE

PLANT TYPE *perennial*
GROWTH RATE *quick-growing*

METHOD *in soil*
LIGHT *low light*

easy

WHAT IT LOOKS LIKE

Lemongrass is an ornamental plant with long, thin, bright green leaves. The stalks are stiff and hard. It is available year-round in Asian markets and some larger supermarkets.

HOW TO GROW IT

Nothing could be simpler. Lemongrass stalks, including bulbs and the leaves, are sold in bunches. Be sure to buy a bunch that has some of the grass blades showing. Place in a tall glass with enough water to cover the bulbous end of the stalk. Put a tablespoon of activated charcoal in the water. (See Starting Plants in Water, page 7.) The roots will start to grow within a week. When the stalks have 2- to 3-inch-long roots, it is time to transplant them.

The supersaturated roots are brittle and should be handled carefully. Cut off the top half of each stalk; the roots are not strong enough to support the full length. Use 6-inch pots filled with very moist potting soil. Make a hole in the soil that is large and deep enough to hold the roots and bulbous end, and plant one stalk in each pot. Keep the plant moist at all times. If you have a garden, transplant the lemon grass as soon as the weather is warm. If you live in the Northern latitudes, you must bring the plant in for the winter.

TIME TO TASTE

You can eat the entire plant. Steep finely chopped leaves to make tea. Crush the bulbous root, much as you would a garlic clove, and add to Asian and Caribbean dishes. Lemongrass is said to relieve headaches and muscle cramps, and aid digestion.

ORIGIN

INDIA. Lemongrass is now grown throughout the sub-tropical world. California and Florida supply the lemongrass market in the United States.

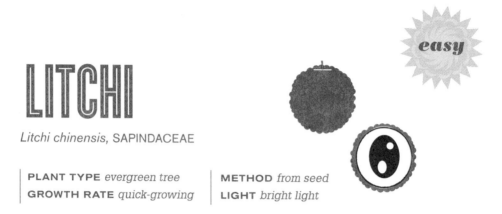

LITCHI

Litchi chinensis, SAPINDACEAE

PLANT TYPE *evergreen tree*	**METHOD** *from seed*
GROWTH RATE *quick-growing*	**LIGHT** *bright light*

WHAT IT LOOKS LIKE

Litchi (also spelled lychee) are round, rosy red fruits with little bumps on them. With its delicate, shiny leaves, the plant is beautiful. Outdoors, the litchi tree grows to a height of 40 feet. Milly had one indoors that grew to a height of 6 feet in about three years. Fresh litchi is available in late spring and early summer in Asian and specialty food markets.

HOW TO GROW IT

Dried and canned litchi nuts can be bought every day of the year in Chinese groceries, but these will not grow. You need to find fresh litchi nuts. To start the seeds, first remove the skin and eat the delicious pulp. Plant the seed in a moistened peat pellet within five days of taking it from the fruit. (See Starting Plants from Seed, page 10.) The seeds should sprout in about two weeks.

Allow the seedlings to grow in the pellets until roots fill the pellet bottoms. At this point, transplant

ORIGIN

SOUTHERN CHINA. The litchi tree has been cultivated in China for more than 2,000 years.

each pellet to a 4-inch flower pot. Fill one-third of each pot with moist potting soil. Place the pellet on the soil, fill in around it, and barely cover it with soil. Place the pots in a bright window.

Time to Taste

Fresh litchi nuts are delicious and quite like the more familiar canned litchis.

LOQUAT

Eriobotrya japonica
ROSACEAE

PLANT TYPE *evergreen tree/shrub*	**METHOD** *from seed*
GROWTH RATE *slow-growing*	**LIGHT** *low light*

WHAT IT LOOKS LIKE

The fruit is pale yellow to light orange with smooth, thin skin. Each fruit is small (1 to 2 inches), round, and sold in clusters. Its flesh bruises easily, but brown spots are not an indication of age or inferiority of fruit. The loquat tree is a lovely symmetrical evergreen. Its new leaves are an attractive woolly gray at first, and then change to a dark glossy green. The leaves on a young tree are typically 4 to 5 inches long; the leaves on a mature plant can be as long as 8 inches. The fruit is available in late spring and early summer in Asian markets and specialty food shops.

HOW TO GROW IT

Each fruit will have one to three large seeds in the central cavity. Wash off any residue of flesh and put the seeds in a sphagnum bag or sow in a flat. Slip a plastic bag over the flat and place it where it will have bottom heat.

The seeds should germinate in two to four weeks. When they do, remove the plastic bag and place the flat in a bright, warm place, avoiding direct sunlight and drafts; plant the sprouted seeds from a sphagnum bag in a small pot. Put in a window with northern light, or put in a light unit. When the seedlings have two sets of leaves, transplant them to 4-inch pots filled with moist potting soil. Make a hole in the pot large and deep enough to hold the roots and insert the seedling. Do not bury any part of the trunk. Put the pots back in a north-facing window or under the lights.

Most loquats will begin to branch at the end of the first year, by which time the plant should be 8 to 10 inches tall. If yours does not branch, pinch the center-growing tip; this will cause new branches to form within a few weeks. In its first few years, the plant grows slowly, but later it may grow up to 2 feet a year.

The loquat is hardy to USDA zone 8 (20°F), and is grown as an ornamental tree in much of the South.

TIME TO TASTE

Loquats are delicious fresh. Their flavor is similar to that of a peach or nectarine. The fruit is canned as a dessert fruit and also used in jams and jellies.

ORIGIN

CHINA AND JAPAN. Today, loquat is cultivated throughout the subtropical regions of the world. In the United States, it is grown commercially in the Gulf region, where it is known as Japanese plum.

Ñame

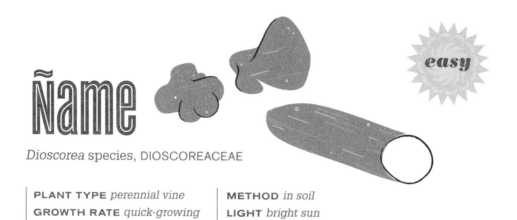

Dioscorea species, DIOSCOREACEAE

PLANT TYPE *perennial vine*	**METHOD** *in soil*
GROWTH RATE *quick-growing*	**LIGHT** *bright sun*

WHAT IT LOOKS LIKE

Ñames come in the most incredible shapes and sizes, some looking like an oversized foot and others like a baseball mitt. These are the biggest of all the tubers, some weighing as much as 6 pounds. The plants are very vigorous vines. The tubers are available year-round in Latin American markets.

HOW TO GROW IT

Start by placing a tuber in a bag containing moist sphagnum moss (see The Secret of the Sphagnum Bag, page 8) and put the bag over heat in a warm, dark place. Check periodically for soft spots, which should be cut away at once because they can cause rot. Do not transplant until the vining stems are 2 to 4 inches long and a healthy root system has developed at the base of the stem.

Select a pot that is 6 to 8 inches across and deep enough to contain the tuber horizontally. Put 1 to 2 inches of moist potting soil in the pot, place the tuber horizontally on the soil (stems up, roots down), and fill in around the tuber with more moist soil, barely covering the top of the tuber. Place in a warm, bright window. Ideally, ñames should be grown in

full sun for the best leaf color, but they do well in any bright location. They need daily watering because of their enormous size.

Once established, ñames can grow at the extraordinary rate of a foot a day. Give them plenty of room and supports on which to trail. A ñame casually left at home for a weekend can strangle a nearby avocado or wrap itself around a television set. Their vigor cannot be over stressed. (You could even use the vines to mask a chain link fence!)

Small new tubers form underground. When Milly and I encountered interesting tuber shapes, we sometimes used the ñames as table decorations. Some, after several months, suddenly started sprouting buds without the aid of soil, heat, or light. (This phenomenon started in May and is probably related to the normal growth cycle of the plant.) When this happened, we reluctantly parted with these *objets d'art* and put them in a sphagnum bag to sprout.

TIME TO TASTE

Ñames are a bit fibrous and tough for North American tastes. Their flavor, however, is similar to that of the sweet potato, and they can be cooked the same way: boiled, peeled, and mashed.

ORIGIN

AFRICA AND ASIA. Widely dispersed throughout the tropical regions of the world.

easy

PERSIMMON

Diospyros kaki, EBENACEAE

PLANT TYPE *deciduous tree*
GROWTH RATE *quick-growing*

METHOD *from seed*
LIGHT *bright sun*

WHAT IT LOOKS LIKE

Persimmons are orange and look somewhat like a tomato. The first leaves of the plant are shiny and pointed, but within a month the mature leaves are veined and bear no resemblance to the young ones. The fruit is available in fall and winter in all markets.

HOW TO GROW IT

Although most persimmons are seedless, the smaller varieties are more likely to bear seeds. The seeds are dark brown, oblong, and at least a ½ inch long. Do not be misled by the tiny black seeds found in the tip of the fruit; these are abortive seeds and will not grow. Persimmons are so delicious, it is not difficult to eat your way through a dozen or so in order to find a few seeds.

To start, extract seeds from the fruit. Stratify them in the refrigerator. (See When "Cold" Is a Good Thing, page 12.) This method should provide 100 percent germination. After removing the seeds from the refrigerator, plant one seed per moistened peat pellet. (See Starting Plants from Seed, page 10.) Slip a plastic bag over the pellets container to insure humidity. Germination takes about two to three weeks. Once the seedlings have sprouted, remove the plastic bag and put the container in a bright window. Persimmon plants grow best with a southern or western exposure.

Young seedlings are ugly ducklings. The stem appears first and is shaped like a loop, but within two weeks it should straighten out and the first leaves should appear. When the plants are 3 inches high, fill one-third of a 4-inch pot with potting soil; place a pellet on the soil and fill in around it with more moist soil.

When a plant reaches 1 foot high, pinch it back to emphasize its naturally rounded shape. The plants must be carefully watered and not allowed to dry out. Grown indoors, the persimmons will not flower, but they can become sturdy little trees. If you have a garden, put plants outside during the warmer months. When they drop their leaves in the fall, bring inside and place in a cool basement or garage. Persimmons are hardy to USDA zone 7b (10°F).

Time to Taste

Persimmons are delicious, but when you buy them in the store, they are rock hard and full of tannin. A trick for ripening the fruits is to put them in the freezer for 24 hours. Remove and thaw and you will have soft, sweet persimmons.

ORIGIN

CHINA. Brought to Japan at an early date, persimmons are very popular in that country today. The Perry Expedition brought them to the United States from Japan. Today, oriental persimmons are grown in California and parts of the South — wherever they can grow in USDA zones 7 to 10.

SUGAR CANE

Saccharum officinarum, POACEAE

PLANT TYPE *annual*
GROWTH RATE *quick-growing*

METHOD *in soil*
LIGHT *bright sun*

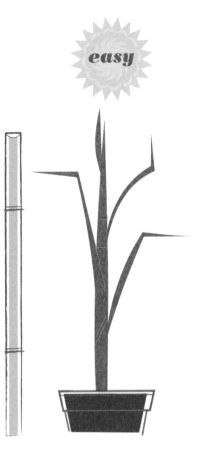

easy

WHAT IT LOOKS LIKE

Sugar cane looks like bamboo. The canes are actually stems with nodes, or rings of root buds. At one side of the ring there is a leaf bud encased in a tiny leaf. The plant produces long, grasslike leaves. Most commercial sugar comes from sugar cane. It is available during the fall in Latin American markets.

HOW TO GROW IT

To start your own sugar cane, ask a Latin American, Asian, or specialty grocer to cut off several pieces for you from the top part of a plant. Each piece should include two nodses. Soak these cuttings overnight, then select a pot big enough to plant them horizontally. Fill one-third of the pot with moist potting soil. Place the cuttings on the soil and cover with about 2 inches of soil. Slip a plastic bag over the pot to retain humidity and put it in a warm dark place.

You can also plant the cuttings vertically. Be sure the buds are pointing up and then bury the cuttings in soil to a point slightly above the bud.

When the cuttings sprout, remove the plastic bag and place the plant in a bright location. Roots and shoots develop from the nodes in two to three weeks. For an effective display, plant half a dozen of these cuttings in a window box. Once established, the plant grows about a foot a month.

Time To Taste

Cut the stalks into short lengths. You can munch on these raw or boil them.

ORIGIN

INDIA, INDOCHINA, AND THE MALAY ARCHIPELAGO. The cultivation of sugar cane spread from India to Europe, and then to the Americas. Columbus carried sugar cane to the West Indies and from there it was brought to the United States. Today, the United States' production of sugar cane is centered mainly in Hawaii and the Southern states.

TAMARIND

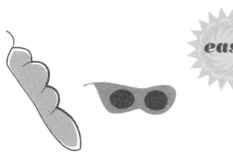

Tamarindus indica, FABACEAE

PLANT TYPE *evergreen tree*	**METHOD** *from seed*
GROWTH RATE *slow-growing*	**LIGHT** *bright sun*

WHAT IT LOOKS LIKE

The cinnamon brown pods are 3 to 8 inches long and resemble large lima bean pods. The tamarind is a large evergreen tree with lovely foliage that closes up at night and unfolds with the first light of day. The foliage has about nine pairs of leaflets and resembles mimosa. The trees develop a slender trunk and grow slowly. Fresh pods are available in spring and summer in Latin American and Asian markets, as well as some specialty food stores.

HOW TO GROW IT

When ripe, the outer pod shell is brittle and is easily peeled back to reveal dark, sticky pulp. Each pod contains three to eight shiny brown seeds. (Frequently, just the pulp is sold in plastic bags as tamarind paste. Poke around to see if you can feel any seeds inside. These seeds are usually viable.) Tamarinds are easily propagated from their seeds. Gently nick the seed's hard

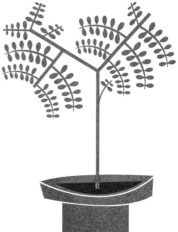

outer shell with a sharp-edged file or piece of sandpaper, and soak the seed until its skin gets crinkled and the seed swells, usually about an hour.

The seeds can be sown in a flat together. Sow them to a depth of 2½ times their size. Slip a plastic bag over the flat and provide bottom heat.

The seeds germinate within two weeks. At this point, remove the plastic bag and put the seedlings in a warm, sunny window. Tamarind seedlings are adorable. Seedpods emerge on rather long, spindly stems. They look like a tiny army of lollipops. A few weeks later, the true compound leaves emerge.

When the leaves appear, transplant the seedlings to individual 4-inch pots that are one-third full of moist potting soil. Place the pots in a sunny window. Keep the soil moist at all times, as a lack of water causes tamarinds to drop their leaves. A well-pruned tamarind grows about a foot a year.

Time to Taste

Tamarind paste, made from the pulp of the pods, is used in curries and many sauces in Indian cooking. The pods can also be steeped to make a delicious, tangy tea. *Beware:* Too much tea can have a laxative effect.

ORIGIN

THE EXACT ORIGIN OF THE TAMARIND TREE IS UNKNOWN, BUT IT IS THOUGHT TO HAVE COME FROM EITHER NORTH AFRICA OR ASIA. Today, it is cultivated throughout the tropics for its edible pods.

TARO

Colocasia esculenta
ARACEAE

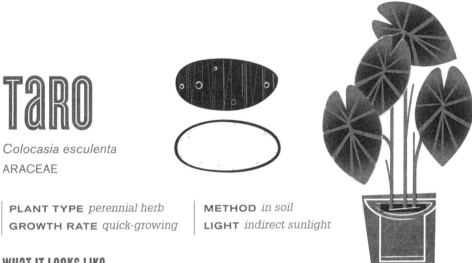

PLANT TYPE *perennial herb*	**METHOD** *in soil*
GROWTH RATE *quick-growing*	**LIGHT** *indirect sunlight*

WHAT IT LOOKS LIKE

Taro is a large, spherical corm that is slightly flattened on top and pointed at the bottom. It is brown in color and has slightly darker horizontal bands circling the corm. A good-sized corm will be 3 to 4 inches across and have incipient (partly formed) pink buds between the horizontal stripes. In nurseries, the corms are sold as ornamental plants called elephant ears because of the shape of the leaves. The corms are available year-round in Asian markets.

HOW TO GROW IT

This is a plant from the tropical jungles of Asia, so it needs high humidity and warmth for germination. Put the corm in a sphagnum bag (see The Secret of the Sphagnum Bag, page 8), seal it, and place in a warm, dark spot. Germination begins within three days. The top buds begin to swell, and soon thick roots sprout

ORIGIN **TROPICAL JUNGLES OF ASIA.** It is an ancient crop.

around the lower three-quarters of the corm. As with all tubers, corms, and bulbs, check every three or four days for any soft spots that might develop and cut these out to prevent rot.

When the roots are 3 inches long, move to a pot that is at least 1 inch larger in diameter than the corm. Put 1 or 2 inches of moist potting soil in the bottom of the pot. Place the corm vertically in the soil and fill in around it, allowing 1 inch of the corm to show above the soil. In its early stages of growth, the corm should continue to have high humidity and bottom heat. After potting, place a plastic bag over the top and put the pot in a bright but not sunny window. Do not remove the plastic until the large central spike that develops is 6 inches high.

Taro is a dramatic performer. Some plants can attain a height of 3 feet within two months. Each corm develops a cluster of large leaves.

Time to Taste

Taro may be served boiled like potatoes, or sliced and deep-fried like potato chips. In Hawaii, taro is the source of the native dish *poi,* a sticky fermented paste made by pounding the boiled taro to a pulp. *Caution:* All parts of the plant are poisonous unless cooked.

WATER CHESTNUT

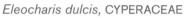

Eleocharis dulcis, CYPERACEAE

easy

PLANT TYPE *perennial corm*	**METHOD** *in soil*
GROWTH RATE *quick-growing*	**LIGHT** *bright sun*

WHAT IT LOOKS LIKE

A round, dark brown corm 1 inch across and about 1 inch high, the water chestnut is flat on the bottom, with one or two small horns or spikes on the top. The plant is aquatic and has long grasslike leaves. It is available year-round in Asian markets.

HOW TO GROW IT

Water chestnuts are very easy to germinate. Select only the firmest, freshest corms. When you get home, put them into a bowl or small bucket of water. Check them periodically for soft spots; if these develop on any of the corms, discard them entirely.

In three to six weeks, white spikes appear at the top of the corms. When the spikes are about 2 inches long, the plants are ready to be transplanted. Use 4-inch pots, each filled with a mixture of three parts potting soil and one part sand

ORIGIN

CHINA. The Chinese have cultivated water chestnuts for their seeds for at least 3,000 years. The seeds are boiled and sometimes sold on the streets as a snack.

or bird gravel. Add one drop of fish fertilizer to each pot, then add water and mix until you have the consistency of mud. The soil should come to the base of the corm's spikes.

Roots will develop at the base of the stem and the old corm will rot away. Cover the soil with a thin layer of pebbles, which will help hold the soil in place. Immerse the pots in a large glass dish containing at least 6 inches of water. Place in a warm, sunny window.

Freshen the water at least once a week to prevent stagnation and supply aeration. To do this, place the glass container under a *gentle* stream of water from the faucet and allow it to overflow for a few minutes. What dirt rises to the top will settle, but be careful not to leave the corms uncovered by soil. You may need to add more soil to your pots from time to time.

The water chestnut grows rapidly, but it is not particularly beautiful. You will soon find you are growing a potful of grass. I once used the plants in an aquarium, and the fish loved the grassy foliage.

Time to Taste

The peeled corms have the texture of a radish and are very sweet. Add water chestnuts to meat and vegetable dishes.

INDEX

A

Achras zapota. See sapodilla
Actinidia sinenesis. See kiwi
activated charcoal, 7
Allium species. *See* garlic;
   onions; shallots
almond, 44–45
Ananas comosus. See pineapple
Anethum graveolens. See dill
anise, 78–79
Annona cherimola. See
   cherimoya
aphids, 16
Apium graveolens. See celery
Arachis hypogaea. See peanut
arrowhead, 122–23
Asian plants, 121–50
Averrhoa camrambola. See
   Chinese star apple
avocado, 46–47

B

bean, 20–21
   sprouting, 22
      beet, 23–24
Beta vulgaris. See beet
bitter melon, 124–25
black sapote, 97–99
bottom heat, 12
Brassica rapa. See turnip
Brassica species. *See* mustard
bulbs, starting, 9
bush bean, 20–21

C

Caesalpinioideae, 48–49
carambola. *See* Chinese star
   apple
caraway, 80–81
Carica papaya. See papaya
caring for plants, 12–15
carob, 48–49
carrot, 25
Carum carvi. See caraway
celery, 82
charcoal, activated, 7
chayote, 100–1
cherimoya, 102–4
chickpea, 26
Chinese red date. *See* jujube
Chinese star apple, 50–51
chocolate pudding tree. *See*
   black sapote
Cicer arietinum. See chickpea
cilantro. *See* coriander
citrus, 52–54
Citrus crassifolia. See Meiwa
   kumquat
Citrus limon 'Ponderosa'. *See*
   Ponderosa lime
Citrus species, 53–54
Citrus × *hystrix. See* Kaffir lime
Citrus × *meyeri. See* Meyer
   lemon
cleaning seeds, 10
cold treatment for seeds, 12
Colocasia esculenta. See taro
commercial light units, 3–4
containers
      for repotting, 13–14
      for starting seeds, 11

coriander, 83–84
Coriandrum sativum. See
   coriander
corn, sprouting, 22
Cucurbita pepo. See summer
   squash
Cymbopogon citratus. See
   lemongrass
Cyphomandra betacea. See
   tamarillo

D

daikon, 126–27
date, 55–56
Daucus carota. See carrot
dill, 85–86
Dioscorea species. *See* ñame
Diospyros digyna. See black
   sapote
Diospyros kaki. See persimmon
dry air, combating, 5

E

Eleocharis dulcis. See water
   chestnut
Eriobotrya japonica. See loquat

F

feijoa, 57–58
Feijoa sellowiana. See feijoa
fennel, 87–88
fenugreek, 89–90
fertilizer, 6
Ficus carica. See fig
fig, 59–60

fluorescent lights, 3–4
Foeniculum vulgare. See fennel
fruiting citrus, 52
fruits, plants from, 43–76

G

garlic, 30–31
genip, 105–6
ginger, 128–29
grapefruit, 53–54
growing techniques, 2–18
growth requirements, 2
guava. *See* strawberry guava;
    tropical guava

H

hand pollination, 86
hardening off of new plants, 13
Helianthus tuberosus. See
    Jerusalem artichoke
herbs, plants from, 77–94

I

Ipomoea batatas. See sweet
    potatoes

J

Japanese plum. *See* loquat
Japanese white radish. *See*
    daikon
Jerusalem artichoke, 27–28
jicama, 107–8
jujube, 130–31

K

Kaffir lime, 52
kiwi, 61–62
knepe. *See* genip
kumquat, 52, 53–54

L

Latin American plants, 95–120
lemon, 52, 53–54
lemongrass, 132–33
Lens culinaris. See lentil
lentil, 29
lighting, artificial, 3–4
light requirements, 2–4
lime, 52
liquid fertilizer, 6
litchi, 134–35
Litchi chinensis. See litchi
loquat, 136–37
lychee. *See* litchi

M

malanga, 109–10
Mangifera indica. See mango
mango, 63–64
mealybugs, 17
Meiwa kumquat, 52
Melicocca bijuga. See genip
Meyer lemon, 52
Momordica charantia. See bitter
    melon
mung beans, sprouting, 22
mustard, 91–92

N

ñame, 138–39
nitrogen, 6
nopales. *See* prickly pear
nuts, plants from, 43–76

O

onion, 30–31
Opuntia ficus-indica. See prickly
    pear
orange, 53–54
outdoor environment for
    plants, 15

P

Pachyrhizus erosus. See jicama
palms. *See* date
papaya, 66–67
pea, 32–33
peanut, 68–69
peat pellets, 11
pebbles, starting plants in, 9
Persea species. *See* avocado
persimmon, 140–42
pests, 15, 16–18
Phaseolus vulgaris. See bean
Phoenix dactylifera. See date
phosphorus, 6
photosynthesis, 2–3
Physalis ixocarpa. See tomatillo
Pimpinella anisum. See anise
pineapple, 70–71
pineapple guava. *See* feijoa
Pisum sativum. See pea
pits, starting, 7
plant lice. *See* aphids
pollination by hand, 86
pomegranate, 72–74
Ponderosa lemon, 52
potassium, 6
potato, 34–35
potting up plants, 5–6, 13–14
prickly pear, 111–13
pruning avocados, 47
Prunus amygdalus. See almond
Psidium guajava. See tropical
    guava
Psidium littorale. See
    strawberry guava
Punica granatum. See
    pomegranate

Q

queenpea. *See* genip

R

radish, 36–37
Raphanus longipinatus. See
    daikon
Raphanus sativus. See radish
repotting, 13–14
requirements for growth, 2
    light, 2–4
    potting mixes, 5–6
    water, 4–5
roots, starting, 7, 9
root vegetables, starting, 9

S

Saccharum officinarum. See
    sugar cane
Sagittaria chinensis. See
    arrowhead
sapodilla, 75–76
scale, 17
Sechium edule. See chayote
seedlings, transplanting, 13
seeds
    bottom heat for, 12
    cleaning, 10
    starting plants from, 8, 10–12
    stratification of, 12
sesame, 93–94
Sesamum indicum. See sesame
shallot, 30–31
shock, 15
soil, 5–6
    starting plants in, 9
Solanum tuberosum. See potato
sooty mold, 18
soybeans, sprouting, 22
Spanish lime. *See* genip
sphagnum moss, 8
spices, plants from, 77–94
spider mites, 18
sprouting
    beans, 22
    corn, 22
    seeds, 12

star apple. *See* Chinese star
    apple
starting plants, 7–11
St. John's-bread. *See* carob
stratification, 12
strawberry guava, 120
sugar cane, 143–44
summer squash, 38–39
sweet potato, 40–41

T

tamarillo, 114–15
tamarind, 145–46
Tamarindus indica. See
    tamarind
tangerine, 53–54
taro, 147–48
tomatillo, 116–17
transpiration, 4
transplanting seedlings, 13
tree tomato. *See* tamarillo
Trigonella foenum-graecum. See
    fenugreek
tropical guava, 118–19
tubers, starting, 7, 8, 9
turnip, 42

V

vegetables. *See also* specific
    kinds
    common, plants from, 19–42
    root, starting, 9

W

water chestnut, 149–50
water requirements, 4–5
water, starting plants in, 7
white fly, 18

X

Xanthosoma sagittifolium. See
    malanga

Z

Zingiber officinale. See ginger
Ziziphus jujube. See jujube

ACKNOWLEDGMENTS

I would like to acknowledge the following people: The members of the Rare Pit & Plant Council (also known as "The Pits"), for their enthusiasm and knowledge while exploring the wonderful world of pits; Stephen Facciola, the author of *Cornucopia,* an invaluable resource about edible plants; Daniel Milkusky, who led us ever so gently into cyberspace; Byron and Laurelynn Martin, owners of Logee's Tropical Plants, for reading the complete manuscript prior to publication and giving feedback.

other Storey titles you will enjoy

The Complete Compost Gardening Guide, by Barbara Pleasant & Deborah L. Martin.
Everything a gardener needs to know to produce the best compost, nourishment
or abundant, flavorful vegetables.
320 pages. Paper. ISBN 978-1-58017-702-3.

Down & Dirty!, by Ellen Zachos.
A fun way for a new generation of gardeners to get started — more than 40 simple
projects to ensure success and build confidence.
256 pages. Paper. ISBN 978-1-58017-641-5.
Hardcover. ISBN 978-1-58017-642-2.

Incredible Vegetables from Self-Watering Containers, by Edward C. Smith.
A foolproof method to produce a bountiful harvest without the trouble of a traditional
earth garden.
256 pages. Paper. ISBN 978-1-58017-556-2.
Hardcover. ISBN 978-1-58017-557-9.

Tabletop Gardens, by Rosemary McCreary.
Designs for 40 dazzling tabletop gardens to inspire the indoor green thumb year-round.
168 pages. Paper with flaps. ISBN 978-1-58017-837-2.

The Veggie Gardener's Answer Book, by Barbara W. Ellis.
Insider's tips and tricks, practical advice, and organic wisdom for vegetable
growers everywhere.
432 pages. Paper. ISBN 978-1-60342-024-2.

Window Boxes Indoors & Out, by James Cramer & Dean Johnson.
Full-color photographs, step-by-step instructions, and quick design ideas for
year-round window boxes.
176 pages. Paper. ISBN 978-1-58017-518-0.

These and other books from Storey Publishing are available
wherever quality books are sold or by calling 1-800-441-5700.
Visit us at *www.storey.com*.